Becoming a Christian

Becoming a Christian

The Ecumenical Implications of Our Common Baptism

Edited by
Thomas F. Best
& Dagmar Heller

Faith and Order Paper No. 184
WCC Publications, Geneva

Cover design: Rob Lucas
Cover photo: The source of the River Jordan (WCC/Dagmar Heller)

ISBN 2-8254-1315-1

150 route de Ferney, P.O. Box 2100,
1211 Geneva 2, Switzerland

Web site: http://www.wcc-coe.org

Printed in Switzerland

Table of Contents

Introduction

THOMAS F. BEST AND DAGMAR HELLER

This book records the reflection and experience of some twenty Christians – liturgists, theologians, church musicians, pastors – who gathered at a Faith and Order consultation held in Faverges, France, in 1997 to struggle with the *implications* of our common baptism for our personal identity as Christians, for the churches and for the ecumenical movement. Why was such a meeting timely, even necessary? And why is baptism so important in the current ecclesial and ecumenical situation? The answers lie in our common experience as Christians and in the ecumenical movement.

A new focus on worship

In recent decades worship has proved to be increasingly significant for the ecumenical movement. Through the liturgical renewal movement which has developed since the 1950s, many churches have discovered a surprising degree of common ground in their understanding and practice of worship. Yet worship is also the place where the divisions among the churches become immediately and painfully evident – and not just at ecumenical gatherings, but also in the life of local congregations. As contacts among local Christians increase, lively and sensitive questions arise about worship, particularly in relation to special liturgical moments such as baptism and the eucharist: Why can my visiting friend from one confession share in our eucharist while another friend, from another confession, cannot? Should we postpone our young children's baptism until they can proclaim "for themselves" their faith in the Lord Jesus? Should a person already integrated within the Christian community be denied the eucharist until he or she has been baptized? And particularly: If the churches do in fact accept one another's baptism, why in some cases do they exclude one another's members from the table of the Lord?

The ecumenical movement itself has brought issues of worship to the fore. Christians from widely differing confessional and historical backgrounds have struggled to find ways of worshipping together which honour and learn from one another's traditions while leaving room for the Spirit to teach and inspire them through new experiences. The phenomenon of worship in ecumenical contexts has stimulated much reflection and creative work by liturgists and church musicians.[1] For its part Faith and Order, not least through the experience of developing worship for its fifth world conference in 1993, has recovered an earlier sense of the centrality of worship in the search for Christian unity. Having focused in the *Baptism, Eucharist and Ministry* process on the *theology* of baptism and the eucharist,[2] we have regained an awareness of these as *acts of worship* within the Christian community, and a renewed sense that we cannot properly understand the meaning of these actions apart from the liturgical practice in which they are embodied.[3]

This fresh perspective already informed the Faith and Order consultation held in Ditchingham, England, in 1994, which explored the pattern or structure (the *ordo*) of Christian worship as increasingly a point of contact and common experience among many churches. Ditchingham also considered criteria for inculturation in worship, and lifted up many practical examples of how worship is fostering the search for unity among churches all around the world.[4] It has been widely regarded as a significant reopening of fruitful contacts between Faith and Order and the community of liturgists, as well as signalling a new sensitivity to the *non-verbal* dimensions of Christian worship.[5]

The same perspective also inspired a meeting in 1995 which took the "Lima liturgy" – the unofficial eucharistic service expressing in liturgical form something of the theological convergence achieved in *Baptism, Eucharist and Ministry* – as a point of departure for fresh consideration of eucharistic worship in ecumenical contexts today.[6] This was not a Faith and Order consultation, but was conducted by persons involved in Faith and Order's work on worship together with the World Council of Churches' worship consultant and the staff of the Ecumenical Institute, Bossey, where the meeting was held. One working group at this meeting developed *Baptism, Eucharist and Ministry*'s simple, unstructured list of "aspects" of the eucharistic service (Eucharist, para. 27) in light of liturgical practice, suggesting which elements are essential to the service, which optional, and how they may be structured and conducted so as best to convey the theological and liturgical meaning of the event.[7] Other groups explored possibilities for inculturation of the eucharistic service, and developed new worship materials for eucharistic services. Thus the gathering contributed decisively to Faith and Order's work on worship.

Baptism: our common bond in Christ

At the Faverges consultation, and thus in this book, Faith and Order turned its attention to baptism as a process fundamental to Christians, to the churches and to the ecumenical movement. In the life-long process of baptism we are instructed in the fundamentals of the Christian faith; we are welcomed, through an act of water-washing in a particular Christian community, into the universal church; and we are nurtured, throughout our life, as we grow into that "life abundant" which is life in Christ. For each Christian, baptism is the portal into new life in Christ: a new life lived in relationship with Christ within the body of Christ, in a local Christian community set within the context of the worldwide church.

Baptism, however, is not only a matter for individuals and particular Christian communities. It concerns also the whole church, and the ecumenical implications of baptism have become central in recent years. Through our common baptism we are all brought into Christ, and this forms the basis of our ecumenical engagement with one another: because Christ has claimed us we have no right to reject one another, whatever our theological, ecclesiological, historical, cultural, social, ethnic and economic differences may be. *Christ's claim is prior* to all earthly sources of both identity and difference, to all the "principalities and powers" of this world, to all the factors within and without the churches which threaten to divide us from one another and to prevent our claiming our birthright to be *one* in Christ Jesus.[8] Since we as Christians are all incorporated into the crucified and glorified Christ, nothing – not even the churches with their centuries of division – can separate us from one another.

This challenges the churches to overcome their continuing divisions, and the churches have responded by stressing baptism as the bond of their unity in Christ. Official mutual recognition of baptism – sometimes stimulated by their engagement with the Faith and Order convergence text *Baptism, Eucharist and Ministry*[9] – now prevails among many Protestant churches. Since the Second Vatican Council the Roman Catholic Church has acknowledged that all "properly performed" baptisms incorporate believers into Christ, and bring them into "a certain, though imperfect, communion with the Catholic Church".[10]

This why is the churches' delegates at the fifth world conference on Faith and Order "affirmed and celebrated together 'the increasing mutual recognition of one another's baptism as the one baptism into Christ'".[11] In recognition of this, many churches are now emphasizing that baptism is baptism into *Christ*, not into this or that historic denomination. In baptism one becomes not a Methodist, Lutheran or Roman Catholic, but a Christian. In some places the churches now signal this by issuing common baptismal certificates, or by sending representatives to accompany and honour baptisms being performed in other churches.

But it is not so simple. Among Protestant churches there are, for example, churches from the Baptist tradition who do not accept the baptism of infants. They require that someone from another Christian church who joins their Christian community be "re"-baptized – or, as they understand, baptized, since in their understanding an act performed without the intentional consent of the person involved is no baptism at all. "Re"-baptism happens also in some Orthodox churches. Strictly speaking, the Orthodox understanding of sacrament means that only baptisms performed within the Orthodox church are valid. Often this principle is applied *kat' oikonomian* (with generous discretion), leading to a "working acceptance" of other baptisms; but where the principle is applied *kat' akribeian* (strictly or literally), "re"-baptism would be practised.[12]

Many have said that the mutual recognition of baptism is central to the modern ecumenical movement. How far do the problems which have been mentioned call this into question?[13]

Another set of issues relates to the understanding and place of baptism within the life of Christians and the churches today. In some situations a particular church is so closely identified with its cultural and historical context that baptism confers not only a Christian identity but also a particular national or ethnic identity. In some situations the social significance of baptism (or the related act of confirmation) seems to overshadow its theological and ecclesial meaning. Other questions relate to the symbolic significance and efficacy of baptism: how do we understand baptism in light of current educational theories, modern understandings of human growth and development, and current thinking about symbolics and ritual action?

Furthermore, every baptism raises the issue of gospel and culture, posing complex questions about the inculturation of Christian faith and ritual actions: How can local practices enhance the process of Christian formation? What are the creative possibilities for local adaptation of the water rite? When must baptism offer a *counter*-cultural witness to society, bringing a Christian critique of local thinking and practice? What are the ethical implications of the process of baptism? What have the churches learned about baptism through and since the process leading to the convergence text *Baptism, Eucharist and Ministry*? And behind these questions stands another: How can the churches face these issues together rather than separately, mutually encouraging – and, where necessary, critiquing and correcting – one another's thought and practice?

Baptism, baptismal practice and Christian unity

For all these reasons and more, baptism is moving to the centre of ecumenical reflection on the life of the churches and on their unity. Following the approach in Ditchingham and Bossey, the Faverges consultation took *liturgical practice*, both historical and contemporary, as an equal partner in the discussion with theology and ecclesiology. Liturgists, theologians and local pastors considered the meaning and ecumenical significance of baptism in light of baptismal practice through the centuries and around the world today.

Notably, our reflections at Faverges were based on an understanding of "baptism" in its broadest sense, as a life-long process including preparation, an act of water-washing and continuing formation in the Christian faith and life. We hope this will ease some discussions among churches which practise the baptism of infants and those baptizing only "believers who can answer for themselves" (report, para. 26, p. 82 below). As at Ditchingham and Bossey, questions of the pattern or structure (*ordo*) of worship and of inculturation were central to the discussion. But Faverges added a new element to the discussion, namely the *ethical* dimension: Christian ethics are those of a community which is entered, and lived in, through the process of baptism including preparation, an act of water-washing and continued Christian formation. How are the meaning of baptism in this broader sense and the symbolism and liturgical practice of the water rite itself *normative* for the nature and practice of Christian ethics?

These aspects of the consultation – its broader understanding of baptism as a life-long process, the emphasis upon actual baptismal practice, the focus on the structure or pattern of baptism as integral to its meaning, the attention to questions of inculturation, the new ethical dimension to the discussion, persistent attention to Christian tradition as well as to contemporary concerns, and the degree to which "believer's baptism" and Orthodox positions were included – are the distinctive features which the Faverges consultation has brought to the ecumenical discussion.

Naturally these need to be seen within the wider ecumenical context, and this book should be read in dialogue with, for example, the study on worship and culture recently conducted by the Lutheran World Federation[14] and the meeting on baptismal theology and Christian unity organized in Helsinki by the Institute for Ecumenical Research, Strasbourg, at the urging of the Lutheran World Federation.[15] We express here our thanks to colleagues in these programmes and institutions for their generous collaboration and support. We repeat our thanks to the presenters and all participants at the Faverges consultation, to its moderator Janet

Crawford, to the staff of the Château de Faverges conference centre and to Carolyn McComish for her work in organizing the meeting and preparing the texts.

The process of baptism is foundational to the life of each Christian, to each church and to the ecumenical movement. May we bring these and all our reflections on baptism to the service of our common Lord, who has through baptism claimed us and made us one.

NOTES

[1] See for example Thomas F. Best and Janet Crawford, "Praise the Lord with the Lyre... and the Gamelan?", in *The Ecumenical Review*, Vol. 46, No. 1, Jan. 1994, pp.78-96, and such collections of worship materials as Per Harling, ed., *Worshipping Ecumenically: Orders of Service from Global Meetings with Suggestions for Local Use*, Geneva, WCC, 1995, and Dietrich Werner et al., eds, *Sinfonia Oecumenica: Worship with the Churches in the World*, Gütersloher Verlagshaus, and Basel, Basileia Verlag, 1998 [in English, German, French and Spanish].

[2] Faith and Order Paper No. 111, Geneva, WCC, 1982. See also Max Thurian and Geoffrey Wainwright, eds, *Baptism and Eucharist: Ecumenical Convergence in Celebration*, Faith and Order Paper No. 117, Geneva, WCC, and Grand Rapids, Eerdmans, 1983, and *Baptism, Eucharist and Ministry 1982-1990: Report on the Process and Responses*, Faith and Order Paper No. 149, Geneva, WCC, 1990.

[3] See Janet Crawford, "Faith and Order Work on Worship: An Historical Survey", and "Worship at Previous Faith and Order World Conferences", in *Minutes of the Meeting of the Faith and Order Standing Commission, 4-11 January 1994*, Faith and Order Paper No. 167, Geneva, WCC, 1994, pp.45-52 and 53-59.

[4] See Thomas F. Best and Dagmar Heller, eds, *So We Believe, So We Pray: Towards Koinonia in Worship*, Faith and Order Paper No. 171, Geneva, WCC, 1995; the letter and report from the consultation also appear in *Studia Liturgica*, Vol. 25, No. 1, 1995, pp.1-31.

[5] For a thoughtful response to the Ditchingham report, see P.J. Naudé, "Regaining our Ritual Coherence: The Question of Textuality and Worship in Ecumenical Reception", *Journal of Ecumenical Studies*, Vol. 35, No. 2, spring 1998, pp.235-56.

[6] Thomas F. Best and Dagmar Heller, eds, *Eucharistic Worship in Ecumenical Contexts: The Lima Liturgy – and Beyond*, Geneva, WCC, 1998. On the "Lima liturgy", see Max Thurian, ed., "The Eucharistic Liturgy: Liturgical Expression of Convergence in Faith Achieved in Baptism, Eucharist and Ministry", Faith and Order Paper No. 116, Geneva, WCC, 1983; also in *Baptism and Eucharist: Ecumenical Convergence in Celebration*, pp.241-55.

[7] *Eucharistic Worship in Ecumenical Contexts*, pp.29-35; this text also appears in *Studia Liturgica*, Vol. 27, No. 1, 1997, pp.94-101.

[8] Cf. the Decree on Ecumenism of the Second Vatican Council: "Baptism, therefore, constitutes a sacramental bond of unity linking all who have been reborn by means of it" (para. 22).

[9] See for example the official response of the Christian Church (Disciples of Christ) to *Baptism, Eucharist and Ministry* in Max Thurian, ed., *Churches Respond to BEM: Official Responses to the "Baptism, Eucharist and Ministry" Text*, Vol. 1, Faith and Order Paper No. 129, Geneva, WCC, 1986, pp.110-21.

[10] Decree on Ecumenism, para. 3: "For men *[sic]* who believe in Christ and have been properly baptized are brought into a certain, though imperfect, communion with the Catholic Church... [despite] many and sometimes serious obstacles to full communion... all those justified by faith through baptism are incorporated into Christ. They therefore have a right to be honoured by the title of Christian, and are properly regarded as brothers in the Lord by the sons of the Catholic Church."

[11] See the report from the Faverges consultation, para. 68 (p. 95 below); the text has also appeared in *Studia Liturgica*, Vol. 29, No. 1, 1999, pp. 1-28. The passage quoted is from the *Worship Book* of the Santiago conference, p.12. See also the report of the Ditchingham consultation, para. 67, in *So We Believe, So We Pray*, p.21.

[12] The dioceses of two Orthodox churches in the German state of Baden-Württemberg joined with seven Protestant churches and the dioceses of the Roman Catholic Church in signing a formal

declaration of mutual acceptance of one another's baptism in 1998. The churches declared together that "... baptism is the bond of unity (Eph. 4:3-6) and establishes communion among all Christians... Our baptism in Christ is 'a call to the churches to overcome their divisions and to make their fellowship visible'." See the account "Gegenseitige Anerkennung der Taufe" [mutual recognition of baptism] published in *Ökumenische Rundschau*, Vol. 48, No. 2, 1999, pp. 253-54. The text of the declaration is available on the web site of the Arbeitsgemeinschaft Christlicher Kirchen in Baden-Württemberg (http://www.kirchen.de/ack/ackbw/rot/taufe.htm).

[13] See Dagmar Heller, "Baptism – the Basis of Church Unity?: The Question of Baptism in Faith and Order", *The Ecumenical Review*, Vol. 50, No. 4, Oct. 1998, pp.480-90.

[14] See S. Anita Stauffer, ed., *Worship and Culture in Dialogue*, Geneva, Lutheran World Federation, Department for Theology and Studies, 1994, esp. the contributions by Gordon Lathrop (pp.17-38), Anscar J. Chupungco (pp.39-56) and S. Anita Stauffer (pp.57-65); cf. also the "Chicago Statement on Worship and Culture: Baptism and Rites of Life Passage", paras 2.1-2.4, in S. Anita Stauffer, ed., *Baptism, Rites of Passage, and Culture*, Geneva, Lutheran World Federation, Department for Theology and Studies, 1998.

[15] See Michael Root and Risto Saarinen, eds, *Baptism and the Unity of the Church*, Grand Rapids, Eerdmans, and Geneva, WCC, 1998.

Becoming a Christian

The Ecumenical Challenge of Our Common Baptism

JANET CRAWFORD

This Faith and Order consultation on "Becoming a Christian: Ecumenical Implications of our Common Baptism" follows on from a consultation on the theme "Towards Koinonia in Worship" held by Faith and Order in Ditchingham, England, in August 1994. Together these two consultations reflect a renewed interest on the part of the Faith and Order commission in the role of worship in the search for the visible unity of the church.

According to its by-laws, the aim of Faith and Order is

> to proclaim the oneness of the church of Jesus Christ and to call the churches to the goal of visible unity in one faith and one eucharistic fellowship, expressed in worship and in common life in Christ, in order that the world may believe (para. 2).

One of the functions of Faith and Order is therefore "to study such questions of faith, order and worship as bear on this task". From the second world conference on Faith and Order (Edinburgh 1937) to the fourth (Montreal 1963), considerable attention was paid to worship, especially to questions of eucharistic worship and intercommunion. During the 1970s, however, Faith and Order work was focused increasingly on development of the convergence text *Baptism, Eucharist and Ministry* (BEM), which was finally published in 1982. Of course BEM treated baptismal and eucharistic theology, but apart from the preparation of the (unofficial) eucharistic liturgy known as the Lima liturgy – which was intended as one possible liturgical expression of the eucharistic theology in BEM – Faith and Order showed little interest in the actual liturgical practice and experience of the churches.[1]

A renewed approach

This situation began to change in the 1990s with the growing realization, expressed in many quarters, that the link between worship and theology – between the *lex orandi* and the *lex credendi* – had become weak in ecumenical discussion, as also in many churches. The importance of once again relating worship to questions of faith and order was emphasized at the fifth world conference on Faith and Order (Santiago de Compostela 1993) and was affirmed by the standing commission on Faith and Order at its meeting in Crêt-Bérard early in 1994.

It was as a result that the Ditchingham consultation was held. The report and other materials from Ditchingham attracted interest from liturgists and theologians as well as pastors and church members.[2] This interest is encouraging, as is the development, since Ditchingham, of a number of links between Faith and Order and bodies such as the Societas Liturgica.

One offshoot of the Ditchingham consultation was a workshop on the Lima liturgy held in May 1995 at the Ecumenical Institute, Bossey. This workshop was organized by Faith and Order staff and the moderator of Faith and Order's study programme on worship, together with the WCC Worship and Spirituality staff and the Ecumenical Institute, Bossey. It brought together some 40 persons from a wide variety of regions and backgrounds, including several of the Ditchingham participants. One result was a paper entitled "Celebrations of the Eucharist in Ecumenical Contexts", which focuses on issues of liturgical practice rather than of text. While this paper, as the product of one group meeting at a workshop, has no official status and is not a Faith and Order paper, it is, nevertheless, a significant contribution to an important topic.[3]

When the Faith and Order board met in Bangkok in January 1996 it agreed that the next step of the work on worship should focus on baptism,

> looking particularly at the actual experience and practice of baptism in the life of the church[es], seeing how it relates to the ecclesiological perspective of churches, and... to theological statements on baptism... [and] how far the ecumenical consensus achieved through BEM is expressed in the liturgical life of the churches.[4]

Baptism: a fresh focus

The mandate was given for a small consultation in 1997, bringing together theologians, liturgists and pastors, with the understanding that this consultation would be complementary to the study being undertaken by the Strasbourg Institute on "baptism and *communio*". Thus although this present consultation at Faverges has its own independent status and significance, it is also part of an ongoing process within both Faith and Order and the wider ecumenical movement. Because of limited resources and last-minute practical difficulties it is smaller than we might have wished, but I believe that we have here sufficient diversity, experience and expertise to produce an important contribution to the study of the ecumenical implications of our common baptism and its liturgical expression in the churches.

The Ditchingham report contains a number of recommendations for further Faith and Order work on worship and I hope that in time the commission will be able to devote attention to most, if not indeed all, of these. The present focus on baptism links with previous Faith and Order work, particularly the major convergence document on *Baptism, Eucharist and Ministry*, to which churches around the world have made an unprecedented response.

The BEM text emphasizes the significance of baptism for koinonia (communion), stating that:

> Through baptism, Christians are brought into union with Christ, with each other, and with the church of every time and place. Our common baptism, which unites us to Christ in faith, is thus a... bond of unity (Baptism, para. 6).

Furthermore,

> Mutual recognition of baptism is acknowledged as an important sign and means of expressing the baptismal unity given in Christ. Whenever possible, mutual recognition should be expressed explicitly by the churches (Baptism, para. 15).

The BEM text continues with a short section on "The Celebration of Baptism" (paras 17-23) which mentions several issues (among them, the symbolic dimension of water, use of the trinitarian formula and the baptizing minister) to which we may want to pay attention. The question of elements necessary for a comprehensive order of baptism (para. 20) will be addressed as one of our major themes, while another major theme will deal with inculturation of baptism (addressed in BEM only in the commentary). Our third major theme, the ethical implications of baptism, develops the statement in BEM that baptism, as a baptism into Christ's death,

> has ethical implications which not only call for personal sanctification, but also motivate Christians to strive for the realization of the will of God in all realms of life (para. 10).

In their responses to BEM the churches generally affirmed the impressive degree of agreement and convergence which exists. Many recognized the importance of the stress in the text on baptism as the primary and fundamental sacrament of unity and the ecumenical implications of this. They approved the sentence which states that "our one baptism into Christ constitutes a call to the churches to overcome their divisions and visibly manifest their fellowship" (para. 6). Points which need further work – and to some of which our consultation may be able to make a contribution – included the biblical basis of baptism, the relationship between baptism and faith, the baptism of believers and infants, contextual challenges, ethical implications and practices which may be interpreted as "re"-baptism.

A number of responses affirmed initiation as a process of life-long growth into Christ, but concern was expressed about a lack of clarity in the meaning of or relation between various parts of the initiation process – water baptism, chrismation, confirmation, admission to the eucharist. There is particular diversity already expressed (in BEM para. 14) over the gift of the Holy Spirit in the initiation process.

The seventh assembly of the World Council of Churches (Canberra 1991) adopted and sent to the churches a statement on "The Unity of the Church as Koinonia: Gift and Calling".[5] While affirming progress that has been made towards visible unity, the statement also notes that "churches have failed to draw the consequences for their life from the degree of communion they have already experienced and the agreement already achieved" (para. 1.3). Among particular challenges to the churches was one "to recognize each other's baptism on the basis of the BEM document" (para. 3.2); such recognition is a significant step towards koinonia given and expressed in "a common sacramental life entered by the one baptism and celebrated together in one eucharistic fellowship" (para. 2.1).

Drawing the consequences

At the fifth world conference on Faith and Order, which focused on the theme "Koinonia in Faith, Life and Witness", delegates affirmed the increasing measure of agreement in the understanding, performance and practice of baptism. The celebration in one of the daily worship services of the increasing "mutual recognition of one another's baptism as the one baptism into Christ" elicited a wide response from the delegates. At the same time they stated that "this very fact invites closer investigation of the conditions on which at least such a minimum of 'mutual recognition' takes place, and of the possibility it suggests of even further consequences to be drawn". In particular, delegates recommended that Faith and Order "put in process for consideration by the churches a way for the mutual recognition of each other's baptism".[6] How might our baptismal liturgies express (and even encourage) such mutual recognition? How is theological convergence towards an understanding of our common baptism into Christ explicitly expressed by the churches in their baptismal practices? These too are questions for us to consider and points at which we may learn from one another's experiences.

The Ditchingham consultation again affirmed the need for further work on baptism, "the event which unites us all into the one body of Christ". The report noted that in spite of changes brought about in response to BEM and to some bilateral dialogues, much work remains to be done to encourage the churches to express the implications of their common baptism more actively in their worship. There was particular interest in the development of a baptismal *ordo*, a liturgical convergence to accompany and help express the growing theological convergence on baptism. Significant work was also done in Ditchingham on the inculturation of worship and the profound issues of unity and catholicity which this raises. Now at Faverges we shall pay attention to both the development of an ecumenical baptismal *ordo* and the inculturation of baptismal liturgies in forms appropriate to specific communities. There were other suggestions made at Ditchingham which I hope we may find time to include in our discussions: shared certificates of baptism, common celebrations of baptism during the Easter vigil, joint construction and use of a font or baptistry, common catechesis and the problems associated with divergences from the traditional trinitarian formula of Father, Son and Holy Spirit.

While there is much work to be done and while we certainly cannot do it all, I hope that in doing what we can we shall help the churches to advance another step towards that visible unity which we believe is Christ's will and Christ's gift.

NOTES

[1] See "Faith and Order Work on Worship: An Historical Survey", *Minutes of the Meeting of the Faith and Order Standing Commission, 4-11 January 1994*, Faith and Order Paper No. 167, Geneva, WCC, 1994, pp.45-52.

[2] The report and other materials appear in Thomas F. Best and Dagmar Heller, eds, *So We Believe, So We Pray: Towards Koinonia in Worship*, Faith and Order Paper No. 171, Geneva, WCC, 1995; the consultation report was also published in a number of journals.

[3] The text and other materials from the consultation appear in Thomas F. Best and Dagmar Heller, eds, *Eucharistic Worship in Ecumenical Contexts: The Lima Liturgy – and Beyond*, Geneva, WCC, 1998, pp.29-35; and in *Studia Liturgica*, Vol. 27, No. 1, 1997, pp.94-101.

[4] *Minutes of the Faith and Order Board, 7-14 January 1996*, Faith and Order Paper No. 172, Geneva, WCC, pp.48-49.

[5] For the text see Michael Kinnamon, ed., *Signs of the Spirit: Official Report, Seventh Assembly, WCC*, Geneva, WCC Publications, and Grand Rapids, Eerdmans, 1991, pp.172-74.

[6] Cf. the report and recommendations of Section III, "Sharing a Common Life in Christ", in Thomas F. Best and Günther Gassmann, eds, *On the Way to Fuller Koinonia: Official Report of the Fifth World Conference on Faith and Order, Santiago de Compostela, 1993*, Faith and Order Paper No. 166, Geneva, WCC, 1994, pp.245-52.

The Water that Speaks

The *Ordo* of Baptism and its Ecumenical Implications

GORDON LATHROP

A sense of the meaning of Christian baptism and of the common shape of its practice throughout the world may be discovered in surprising places. For example, we may find this meaning obliquely in a classic text from the history of the church which is not about baptism at all, but which only indirectly reflects baptismal practice or uses baptismal imagery. Sometimes, however, the very surprise of such a discovery and the character of its context may disclose to us in clarity the vibrant importance of the basic pattern of baptizing.

Thus, early in the 2nd century of our era, Ignatius, bishop of Antioch, on his way towards trial and martyrdom, wrote the following text to the Christians of Rome, the city where he was finally to die. He wrote, not about baptism, but about his impending death:

> Do not speak Jesus Christ yet set your heart upon the world... My desire (*eros*) has been crucified and there is not in me any fire which feeds off material stuff (*pyr philoulon*), but rather there is water living and speaking in me, saying to me from within, "Come to the Father." I do not delight in the food of death nor the pleasures of this life. I want the bread of God, which is the flesh of Jesus Christ, descended from David, and I want the drink of his blood, which is deathless love (*agape*).[1]

With this remarkable text, Ignatius characterizes the martyrdom he expects and for which he longs, using the imagery of the central matters of the Christian community: the word of God, the water of new birth into the body of Christ, the love-feast of the eucharist. Of course, these primal words – water, speaking, bread, flesh, drink, blood, love – have multiple meanings, including multiple religious meanings. But here, in his writing to another church, an assembly marked by these very things used together, their central Christian liturgical meanings cannot be far away from the sense which Ignatius intends. He seems to wish to convince the Roman church that he does indeed choose to drink the cup which his

Lord drank, to be baptized with the baptism with which his Lord was baptized (cf. Mark 10:38-39). He thereby wishes to prevent that church's expected efforts on his behalf. Indeed, he has already said that if he is able to die bearing witness to the Christian faith, he will be "word of God" spoken for others to hear, not just another "cry" evaporating in the needy history of the world.[2] He has already argued, using strong baptismal analogies, that his death will be a birth, an illumination, a patterning after the passion of Christ.[3]

It should be no surprise that baptism and eucharist could function in the ancient church as *metaphors* for suffering witness before the world as well as *sources* for such ethical action, for they already functioned this way in the gospel of Mark. They continued so to function in the church of the martyrs.[4] In a cruel and oppressive time, the distance between eating the bread of God in the community and being "ground as wheat" in the arena was not long.[5] But it may surprise us to note that even in such an impassioned text, in such an existentially charged situation, the bishop of Antioch presents his metaphor in what might be regarded as an *ordo*. On this view, he is becoming a martyr in a way exactly analogous to the way he has seen many other people become Christians, a way surrounded by the assembly in the midst of which he has *presided*.[6] So now he, the bishop, is the one who, having heard the community "speaking Jesus Christ", has left behind the ways of "this life", renouncing "the ruler of this world" and the fire and food of death, in order to turn towards God through that same Jesus Christ.[7] He, the bishop, has been brought again to the water and the word, though now to the water that speaks from within, in his *memory*, in words that continue to insert him into the very life of the triune God, in water that is the very outpoured Spirit of God within him (John 4:14; 7:37-39; 19:34). And now through that water he, the bishop, turns to the communal meal of God which is the very sharing in Christ's suffering in the flesh, the telling of the truth of all-transforming love. He is doing all of this – turning from evil, listening to the speaking water, turning to the meal – openly, in the clear sight of the communities of the churches to which he writes, through whose towns he passes. Ignatius is in the midst of the process of becoming a martyr, a process he sees as reflecting that of becoming a Christian.[8]

Proclamation and conversion, the speaking water, the meal: such was likely the *ordo* of the making of Christians in Antioch. And this *ordo* was then available to be remembered, again and again. Even more profoundly, this *ordo*, this one baptism, could be understood as having occurred "once for all" in Christ, as continually co-extensive with all authentic, witnessing Christian life. One was to live through this pattern repeatedly, not repeating the water-washing but listening to its "voice", acting on its invitation. Furthermore, although this *ordo* could be taken to reflect the practice which Ignatius would have known at Antioch, he could also expect it to be understood at Rome: in these central matters the churches were at one.

Indeed, the text is a remarkable example of a 2nd-century meaning of "church" which may be helpful to us today. The local church of Antioch is in communion with the local church in Rome. Both places share the patterns of the "speaking water" (that is, the water conjoined with the voice of God) and the meal of God. Between these churches (in fact, literally, geographically, *between* them), the strikingly self-conscious – even seemingly *modern* – "I" of the speaker acts in a pattern he has received from the liturgical life of his own community[9] with a trust in the recognition which will be there in the community towards which he is going.[10] Christians are gathered in a local *personal*-communal assembly, in communion with other personal-communal assemblies, in which mutual understanding is enabled by the common experience of the nearness of the triune God and of conformity in faith and life to the pattern of Christ's cross and resurrection, and by the shared *ordo*, the mutually recognizable great pattern, of baptism, eucharist and ministry.

We may rightly find ourselves troubled by what seems to be Ignatius's enthusiasm for martyrdom and his world-denying piety. We may prefer Polycarp's greater wisdom of reluctance. Yet Ignatius is one of the very early voices to insist on the materiality, the *flesh*, of Christ. Even here he is not escaping the stuff of the material world – water and food and flesh, for example. Rather, he is seeing it reoriented from death towards God and life. Furthermore, about the actual circumstances of his arrest and death we know very little and cannot judge. We only know his stunning imagery. The doubts, the foreignness, the distance from late-20th-century devotion remain. But in the present ecumenical conversation we may also find great gifts for our work in the hints this text gives of the *ordo* of Christian baptism as it was known at Antioch, and in Ignatius's sense of its continual and urgent theological and ethical significance.

Can we too speak together about the baptismal *ordo* of our own local churches in ways that are mutually recognizable? And can we do so with similar passion for the theological, ecumenical and ethical meanings of that *ordo*? Can we understand together how baptism – baptism in its process, baptism with its continual echoes in the Christian life, baptism in its unifying work among the churches – may be "word of God" and not simply a "cry" amidst the need of the present world?

The Ditchingham *ordo*

In fact, much greater attention seems to have been given recently to the *ordo* of the eucharist as an ecumenical inheritance and as an instrument of *koinonia* than to the order or pattern of baptizing. The classic study of the developing pattern of eucharistic celebration, widely influential in ecumenical liturgical conversation, was that of Dom Gregory Dix.[11] The Lima document on *Baptism, Eucharist and Ministry* presented its account of the elements of eucharistic liturgy in a widely recognizable sequence or pattern (cf. Eucharist, para. 27). A great variety of churches have recently used an *ordo* for eucharist – a pattern marked, indeed, by considerable mutual convergence – as the way to present and organize their own liturgical materials.[12] And one recent consultation on the future use of the Lima liturgy made a strong proposal for an *ordo* of eucharist as a pattern for ecumenical celebration and for local inculturation and local unity.[13] In many ways this proposal built on the work of the earlier consultation on the role of worship in the search for Christian unity held in Ditchingham, England, in 1994. That gathering, in its report, had already given a central place to the ecumenical significance of the pattern of eucharistic celebration.[14] But the Ditchingham consultation also suggested that baptism itself has an order and pattern that is meaningful, ancient and increasingly recognized in the churches.

The consultation report says this about pattern in worship:

> The liturgy of Christians occurs in assembly; it also occurs in the midst of daily life in the world... The pattern of this gathering and sending has come to all the churches as a common and shared inheritance. That received pattern resides in the basic outlines of what may be called the *ordo* of Christian worship, i.e. the undergirding structure which is to be perceived in the ordering and scheduling of the most primary elements of Christian worship. This *ordo*, which is always marked by pairing and by mutually reinterpretive juxtapositions, roots in word and sacrament held together...

There follows a discussion of the eucharistic *ordo*. But then the report uses these sentences:

> It is formation in faith and baptizing in water together, leading to participation in the life of the community. It is ministers and people, enacting these things, together.... Such is the inheritance of all the churches, founded in the New Testament, locally practised today, and attested to in the ancient sources of both the Christian East and the Christian West. (Ditchingham, paras 3-4).

According to Ditchingham, this *ordo* of Christian worship, including the deep pattern of baptizing, is to be dealt with as a gift, not a demand (para. 5). Along with the other materials of this *ordo*, the water of baptism is to be celebrated as a connection between faith and life, gospel and creation, Christ and culture (para. 6). Furthermore, the juxtaposed matters "of catechetical formation and baptism" are among those "principal pairs of the Christian liturgy" which "give us a basis for a mutually encouraging conversation between the churches", for inculturation, for renewal, for attention to each other's charisms, for local unity (paras 7-8). Indeed, the very duality of this *ordo* may help us overcome old disputes:

> The *Baptism, Eucharist and Ministry* document is itself a model of such discussion of classic points of division in the light of shared liturgical patterns. Thus, for example, when baptism is seen to be a process of both faith-formation and water-washing, believer baptist groups may be able to see themselves as enrolling their young children in a catechumenate, recognizable to many other Christians, while infant-baptizing groups may find their own life-long call to discipleship and learning refreshed, and both groups will find themselves called to a strong celebration of baptism which shows forth its centrality and meaning. Future Faith and Order discussions could well be formed according to this model, with liturgical studies a welcome partner in the conversation (Ditchingham, para. 11).

So the "Ditchingham *ordo*" includes baptism, in a very simple way. It outlines the baptismal event as two things, "formation in faith" and "water-washing", side by side, leading to a third thing, "participation in the life of the community". Does this correspond with what we have seen in Ignatius? Yes, if we see that "formation in faith" includes both "speaking Jesus Christ" and renouncing the ways of evil and death. Yes, if we see also that the "words" which belong to formation in faith, to teaching and learning, are also alive and continued in the water-event itself, saying, in the power of the Spirit, to the one who is baptized into Christ's death: "Come to the Father." Yes, if we understand that the "voice" which Ignatius hears through the interior, remembered water, says nothing else than what he has heard in the word of God throughout his Christian life. Yes, if we see that Ditchingham, leaning on the Lima document, understands that the baptismal *ordo* has life-long significance. Yes, if we see that the "meal of God", in both of its senses – as celebration in the assembly and as sharing in the cup of Christ through suffering witness in the world – is the primary form of "participation in the life of the community". Yes, if we see that the water leads to that meal, and the meal tells the truth about the world as it is before God.

In rough schematic form, the Ditchingham *ordo* for baptism is:
formation in faith;
water-washing;
participation in the life of the community;

though the life-long call to learning and discipleship also places the continued formation in faith *after* the water. The pattern we may discern in Ignatius shows the same outline:

proclamation, conversion, turning from evil;
the "speaking water";
the meal of God/witness in the world.

Of course, the very fact that we may discern the pattern in his account of his own potential death is a testimony to Ignatius's view of the life-long significance of the baptismal process.

But can we discover this shape of baptism elsewhere? Is it discoverable in actual liturgical evidence, not just in allusion? Is it present in the earliest centuries of the church? Indeed, is it present in the New Testament itself? Finally, is it present in our communities? And, if it is, does such a simple outline help us in our tasks of mutual recognition and mutual encouragement?

Justin and other early models

In fact, there is a striking correspondence between this pattern and what we may discover in the work of Justin, a layman or catechist who was teaching in Rome about four decades after Ignatius would have been killed there. We have in Justin's work the first full direct description which we possess of what happens in Christian baptism. The description occurs in Justin's first *Apology*, a defence of Christian faith and practice addressed to the Roman emperor of that time, Antoninus Pius. Intended as a defence, the description is inevitably truthful, schematic, non-technical and interested in meaning – all of which makes the account of high value for us.

Towards the end of his work, Justin writes:

> We shall now also explain the way in which we dedicated ourselves as votive gifts to God, having been made new through Jesus Christ, lest in omitting this we should appear to do something wrong in our explanation. As many people as are persuaded, as believe these things taught and spoken by us to be true, and as promise to try to live thus, are taught to pray and ask God, while fasting, for the forgiveness of sins, while we pray and fast together with them. Then they are led by us there where water is, and they are reborn in the way of rebirth with which we ourselves were reborn. For they then do the washing in the water in the name of the Father and Lord God of all things and of our Saviour Jesus Christ and of the Holy Spirit... And this washing is called illumination, since the understanding of those who learn these things is illuminated... But, after thus washing those who are persuaded and who assent, we lead them to those who are called brothers and sisters, where they are assembled to make common prayer with strength for themselves and for those illuminated and for all others everywhere... When we have ended the prayers, we

> greet one another with a kiss. Then the brothers and sisters set out before the president bread and a cup of mixed wine...

Following an account of the eucharist and of the meaning of the gift of the body and blood of Christ in the eucharist, Justin continues:

> And for the rest, after these things we continually remind each other of these things. Those who have the means help all those who are in want, and we continually meet together. And over all that we take to eat we bless the Creator of all things through God's Son Jesus Christ and through the Holy Spirit. And on the day named after the sun, all, whether they live in the city or the countryside, are gathered together in unity...[15]

There follows an account of the Sunday eucharist, of the sending of communion to the absent and food and support to the poor, and of the meaning of Sunday. So the book, the defence of the faith, ends.

We could summarize this baptismal process with the very pattern we found in Ignatius, echoed at Ditchingham: *formation* in the faith or conversion; the *washing* with water associated with the word and name of the triune God; and *participation* in the life of the community, including now the continual mutual remembrance of baptism, the remembrance of the poor, the communal meetings, the meal-thanksgiving and, as the event which incorporates all of this, the Sunday eucharist. We can also say that several things which are implicit in Ignatius are made quite explicit here. Proclamation and teaching precede the water, but they also follow; indeed, a "continual reminding" is a strong part of the *ordo*. The baptismal events occur in the community and lead to participation in the community's life; the meal is at the centre of such participation.

Such life-long meaning of baptism and such communal resonance are obviously present in Ignatius too. But in Justin the whole matter is set in motion, even in *procession*, and accompanied by prayer. The resultant pattern could be listed in this way:

teaching the faith and enquiry about conduct;
praying and fasting of candidates and community;
procession to the water;
washing;
procession to the place of community prayer;
eucharist;
continual reminding, in Sunday eucharist and in care of the poor.

It is of considerable interest that, armed with this pattern, we can discover something like the same *ordo* in the (probably earlier) Syrian book the *Didache* or "The Teaching of the Twelve Apostles". If we assume that this ancient "church order" begins with catechesis for those who are coming to be baptized, the resultant order of the book is strongly familiar.[16] There the pattern is:

moral instruction (1:1-6:3);
fasting and prayer (7:4-8:3; "before the baptism", 7:4);
baptism in the triune name in "living water" (7:1-3);[17]
eucharist after baptism (9-10);
the life of the community, including reception of travelling teachers (11-13), giving to the poor (13:4), the every-Sunday eucharist (14).

In fact, this primitive order for making a Christian ultimately becomes the order of the "catechumenate", known to us from many sources from the 3rd century on:

enquiry about willingness to change conduct;
hearing the gospel/teaching the words for faith;
prayer (and fasting);
washing;
leading to the meal,
to "mystagogy", the learning of the mysteries in which one was now participant;
and to the resultant weekly assembly, witness and care for the poor.

Such a process came to be associated with the Christian keeping of *pascha* and thereby to influence profoundly the evolving shape of Lent and Easter. This process itself was ultimately represented by the developed form of the Western Christian "catechism", in which specific central texts came to stand as symbols for parts of the process, as gifts which had been given to those being baptized and could now be repeated as ways of continual reminding, continual re-insertion in baptismal faith:

the ten commandments;
the creed;
the Lord's Prayer;
baptism (e.g., the Great Commission, Matt. 28:16-20);
holy communion (e.g., the *verba institutionis*);
confession and forgiveness/daily prayer/duties.

Furthermore, our 3rd-century witnesses (the *apostolic Tradition*, Tertullian, the *Acts of Thomas*) begin to show that at this time some ritual signs of the outpouring of the Spirit in baptism – or some signs that the baptized were being made a people of priests and kings – were being added to the process, in different places and with slightly differing meanings. The most frequent such sign was the anointing with oil. We do not really know the age or provenance of this practice. Was it drawn from the mysteries or from gnosticism? Was it an intentional addition of an impure agent (oil) to the bath of purity, in order to sign the radical new meaning of that bath in Jesus Christ? Was it a sign of hospitality and welcome, drawn to baptismal practice from meal practice or from the use of the baths? Was it simply an enacting of the biblical words about the Spirit? Or was it all of these and more? Regardless of any favourite theory, it is important to note that this anointing comes to interpret the process itself, to mark its movement, as a new Christian is brought from "darkness" into the "priestly people of God", not to be another thing altogether, not to create a new structure.

The 3rd century also begins to show evidence of the baptism of "those who cannot answer for themselves". Here too, however, the basic structure of baptism remains the same. Teaching and formation in the faith are given to those who bring the children, those who answer for them, prior to the bath. The children are welcomed into the life of the community. Indeed, the 3rd-century evidence about such baptized children shows that they were also brought to participation in the eucharist. And the pattern of "continual reminding" was, of course, exactly what was called for in the ongoing catechesis of baptized infants.

It is also important to note that the root structure – faith formation, speaking water, communal participation – could be unfolded in very different ways already in the ancient world. In Syrian Christianity and subsequently in Armenian Christianity, for example, there is evidence of slightly different accents, a different role for the community and great importance for post-baptismal instruction.[18] The primitive pattern here could be summarized as follows:

a conversion takes place, miraculously, sometimes in encounter with a lone apostle;
the apostle prays for the convert(s);
a seven-day fast occurs;
on the eighth day there occurs anointing of the head, bath, eucharist;
followed by introduction to the community and instruction in ethics.

Of course, such a baptism looks rather more like the baptism of the Ethiopian eunuch (Acts 8) or the order of Matthew 28 – "baptizing them" followed by "teaching them to obey" – than the baptisms of the day of Pentecost (Acts 2). But even here the core structure, although weighted differently, is the same: encounter-proclamation-conversion-formation in faith leads to water bath, leads to meal-communal life-further instruction.

The New Testament

Does this core structure itself have a biblical origin? Can we find it in the scripture? Of course, the New Testament is not a book of rituals. Nor does it give clear evidence on ancient Christian practice. But to the extent that such evidence can be gathered indirectly, the deep pattern here is also the same. This root pattern may in fact be seen in widely divergent parts of the New Testament. Thus, the baptisms of the day of Pentecost (Acts 2:42) follow from Peter's preaching and lead those baptized to "devote themselves to the apostles' teaching and fellowship, to the breaking of bread and the prayers" (Acts 2:42), as well as to distribution of goods "to all, as any had need" (Acts 2:45). Indeed, Paul depends on Christian baptism leading to the meal for his analogy with the crossing of the sea leading to eating the manna and drinking from the rock (1 Cor. 10).

Furthermore, if 1 Peter may be considered to be a baptismal catechesis and a church order, there too the order of making Christians is the same. Proclamation of the resurrection and teaching about ethical transformation (1:3-21) lead to "purification" (1:22) and "new birth" (1:23). This purification through the word of God – which may be a reference to the water-bath – leads in turn to communal love (1:23; 2:1); to eating and drinking (2:2-3); to participation in the community, the royal priesthood, the people of God (2:4-10); and to moral instruction (2:11ff.). The order of 1 Peter can also be seen to be formed by the process of the baptismal *ordo*.[19]

That such an order is significant, that it is not simply the self-evident way that baptisms might be done, can be gathered from the washings which may have surrounded the origin of Christian baptizing.[20] Several 1st-century groups seem to have practised a full-body washing, in running or deep water, for the sake of ritual purity and in order to be ready for – even to compel – the coming day of God. Amid such washings, John's baptism seems to have functioned as an astonishing proclamation of the nearness of the reign of God through the prophetic sign he enacted when *he* did the washing rather than encouraging others to bathe themselves. John the *baptizer* signed the nearness of the God who would come to wash a people of God's own.[21]

Like these washings, Christians also washed with water towards the coming day of God. Like John's baptism, the Christian bath was not self-administered. But unlike all of these washings, Christian baptism was not repeated. And it was finally not about *purity*. Its eschatology was new and surprising. It led to participation in Jesus Christ, to death and resurrection, hence to what was regarded as "unclean", to the meal of his body and blood, to engagement with the poor and the outsiders, not to a pure life cut off from others. It was not about personal purity but communal participation in Christ. It led to the day of God by incorporating the baptized into the community which tasted the down-payment of that day in the presence of the crucified-risen one and in the Spirit that was poured out from his cross and resurrection. It was itself an eschatological reality by being drawn into the very life and name of the triune God. All the many images and meanings for baptism in the New Testament – washing for the wedding, illumination, forgiveness, entering the temple, surviving the flood, being clothed in Christ – can be taken as celebrations of this eschatological reality.

Every baptism into Christ thus participates in the meaning of the stories of the baptism of Jesus himself (Mark 1:9-11 and parallels): the candidate goes into the water with Christ, the Spirit descends and the voice of the Father calls this one a beloved child, a participant in the body of Christ.[22] Such is baptism "in the name of the Father and of the Son and of the Holy Spirit" (Matt. 28:19). But the Christian arises from these waters not to fasting and temptation – the foreshadowing of Jesus' cross which follows the Jordan story – but to participation in the meal and mission of Christ. And every baptism into Christ participates in the meaning of the stories of his death and resurrection, his final "baptism" (Mark 10:38; Luke 12:50). The candidate is buried in these waters together with Christ, in order to be raised with him. The Christian arises from these waters to participation in the world-changing, witnessing, communal meal with the risen one and those who are in him. Christian baptism is therefore not a purity-rite which can be repeated and repeated. Christian baptism is an event in the name of God, filled with the presence of God (Matt. 28:20). Unlike the surrounding washings, then, Christian baptism called for teaching and formation in that name. And it led to remembering the meaning of this new washing and teaching its ethical consequences. The new character of *this* washing could be expressed by *this ordo*: teaching, washing, community participation – or, put differently, conversion, the speaking water, the meal. This washing was henceforth "water that speaks" with the voice of God, not simply our own cry for help. This washing was henceforth in water that had been itself washed by Jesus Christ and so by the triune God.

Thus it needs to be noted that "baptism in the name" did not always mean that a formula like those in Matthew 28:19 and Acts 2:38 was actually recited over the use of the water. Such a conception gives far too small a meaning to the phrase. It seems unlikely that this phrase in the New Testament refers to the "recitation of a formula" (cf. 1 Cor. 1:13-15). Furthermore, we have clear evidence of early baptisms where no such formula existed.[23] While the recited name has come to function at Christian baptism in a foundational way, the use of such a text is actually a symbol which condenses the whole *ordo*. Baptism in the triune name involves learning to trust in God by being washed into the crucified Christ and being raised to live in the community of the Spirit. The *ordo* is itself trinitarian. The *ordo* stands for the name.

Baptism in the triune name is none other than that one washing which is no longer a purity rite, a prayer for God, a cry for help, but rather a participation in the very life of the present God of the gospel, the God seen at Jordan, known in the resurrection, poured out as the Spirit. The "name" is both the content of the teaching which must be juxtaposed to the washing and the powerful presence of the gracious God who makes of our water the very threshold of the eschatological day.

Baptism in the name of Jesus Christ, baptism in the triune name and baptism in the Spirit are thus exactly the same thing: an ancient human water-rite transformed to be the making of Christians-in-community. They are the making of Christians done in such a way that the act itself becomes a life-long pattern of living.

In the New Testament, therefore, baptism is no distinction from the rest of needy humanity. It is rather open identification with all in Jesus Christ and in the mission which is through him. It is the washing which makes Christians to be "unclean" with Christ, who welcomes the impure (Mark 2:15) and the unwashed (Mark 7:2) and the unclean (John 4, 5, 9) and the dead (John 11). It is the bath which constitutes his witnesses in the world.

The water that speaks: implications

So the *ordo* of baptism can be stated this way: teaching, bath, meal. Or this: formation in faith, the water that speaks, participation in the communal witness to God's new age. Three implications follow.

1. This ordo may give us a key for a fresh ecumenical reading of the Lima document and of the responses of the churches to it.

It is no surprise that the Lima document should breathe much of the same spirit we have discovered in the New Testament and in Justin and Ignatius. It is not so much that its account of a "comprehensive order of baptism" (Baptism, para. 20) corresponds to the *ordo* we are perceiving here. The matters listed in that paragraph are useful, but they are not yet a very profound or full reflection of the *ordo*, unless it is seen that scripture, the Spirit, renunciation and profession have led to the water, and that new identity, membership in the church and witness continually follow. The matters present in the moment of baptismal celebration must be seen as recapitulating the entire process. Rather, our reflections find an echo and reinforcement in the document's sense of the eschatological meaning of baptism (Baptism, para. 7), in its rich biblical imagery (paras 2-6), in its sense that baptism is repeatedly affirmed and has life-long significance (para. 9), and in its reflection on the ethical significance of baptism (para. 10). Most of all, our *ordo* corresponds most profoundly to the document's assertion that baptism is a *process* (commentaries on paras 12 and 14) which takes place within the *community* of the church (paras 6, 12, 23).

It is in such reflections on baptism that the Lima document invites us to receive *ourselves*,[24] to say Amen to a reality that we already have and that we already share. Indeed, many of the responses of the churches to the Lima document recognize the ways in which BEM has encouraged them to recover practices and meanings which belong almost instinctively to the deepest charism of the churches themselves: that baptism is a process, a continuum, as well as a once-for-all event;[25] that catechesis and proclamation belong to baptism; that baptism involves the strong, identity-changing use of water; that baptism takes place in the assembly and leads to participation in community and life-long witness. Such recognition reflects a deep awareness that the *ordo* we have been discussing is present in the churches. And such recognition has led Christians of one church to the awareness of the presence of the same recovered pattern in other churches as well. We are invited to find in each other the living, trinitarian pattern of the baptized, just as the Roman church was invited to recognize that same pattern in Antioch through the person of Ignatius.

It is certainly true that other matters discussed in the responses of the churches and implied in our discussion of the *ordo* could be more clearly expressed than they are in the Lima document. The *word* present in the baptismal process and in the celebration of baptism itself ought not to be only "the scriptures referring to baptism" (Baptism, para. 20), but a reading, teaching and preaching of all the scriptures as filled with the triune "name". The word which comes to the water includes all the preaching of the church.[26] Furthermore, a strong *catechumenate* should be encouraged among the churches though, as in the ancient Syrian church, that catechumenate may take very different forms. And the life-long meaning of baptism could be further elaborated by a discussion of the baptismal shape of *repentance and forgiveness* or *reconciliation* in the church,[27] of *vocation* and work and Christian ministry, of human *life and suffering*,[28] of Christian *witness* and the continuing content of Christian *faith*,[29] and, finally, of human *death* itself.

2. This ordo can also propose to us concrete possibilities for the renewal of our baptismal practice.

The point of our conversations is not to amend the Lima document, but rather to proceed with mutual recognition and renewal. It is to enquire whether the presence of the *ordo* in the churches, the *ordo* which we can discern as behind the Lima document and available from our common sources, can be clarified and refreshed in our own actual practice. Can we actually hold together baptism and formation in the faith? Can we welcome again the ministry of catechists and baptismal sponsors in our midst? Can we see the creeds as baptismal symbols, central doctrines as having baptismal locus? Can we teach a living trinitarian faith, based on the churches' experience of the triune God in the "speaking water"? Can we practice a strong use of the water, recovering immersion fonts where possible? Can we see the events of the actual baptismal celebration as recapitulating the whole process of baptism, indeed the whole Christian life? Can we let any strong secondary symbols used in the rite – prayer over the water, oil, light, new clothing or other symbols adapted from diverse cultural surroundings – function to unfold the meaning of the *ordo* itself? Can we let the whole assembly – or as many of its members as possible – gather around our fonts (or at rivers, lakes or oceans), welcoming the newly baptized into the community and to participation in the eucharist? Can we bring all the baptized, including the children, directly to the meal of God? Can we enable a "life-long catechumenate", a continual re-learning of the faith, a continual re-hearing of the voice in the water? Can we actually connect baptism and ethics, baptism and mission? Can we unfold this whole *ordo* in each local place in ways appropriate to the dignity and gifts of that place? And can we do these things by teaching, love and invitation, by opening up what is already present in the churches, not by constraint and compulsion?

And, to press the questions even more deeply, can we let the Lund Principle be applied here?[30] Are there not many of these things that we can indeed do together? Could a renewed catechumenate be undertaken together? Could we be present at each other's baptisms? Could we do baptisms on the great feasts and do them side-by-side? Could we even consider constructing a single font for the local churches in our towns and cities (cf. Ditchingham, para. 12)?

The actual liturgy for the baptism itself, in all of our churches, may then most wisely include these things: the presence of the local church, including the ministerial leadership of that community and witnesses from the larger *koinonia*; a recapitulation of the process which has led to the water, including the confession of trinitarian faith by the community, by the candidates and by the sponsors of those who cannot answer for themselves; prayer; as full a washing with water as possible; a testimony to the new identity of the baptized in communion with both the local church and the whole catholic church; and a direct flow into the eucharist and mission.

This *ordo* which has been present in our reflections and which hovers behind the Lima text can be interpreted as holding together several matters which have been torn apart in the history of baptism. Such matters include: catechesis and bath, water and meal, faith and gift, speech and sign, adults and children, individual salvation and communal meaning, present and future, one-time-event and all of life, baptism and confirmation, the local church and the universal church, the present community and the ancestors in the faith, God's action and the church's action. With contemporary liturgical studies, with the Lima document, with experiments in the catechumenate, with liturgical books influenced by BEM, with new baptismal ethics, with reflections on baptism as *process*, and with local efforts at renewed baptismal practice, the churches are about the task of re-membering this dismemberment.

3. This ordo which we are discussing may assist us to re-address, with a new wholeness, old points of Christian division.

For example, when baptism is a process, the disagreements between "baptists" and "catholics" may be turned into mutual admonition and mutual enrichment (cf. Ditchingham, para. 11). Furthermore, when the central event of the *ordo* is a *bath*, we all may yield the practical point of immersion to the "baptists". We may encourage and rejoice in the fullest possible use of water while, in the spirit of the ancient *Didache*, not enforcing this legalistically.

Moreover, when adult Christians are always, like the bishop of Antioch himself, still becoming real Christians, when the word alive in the water is always still speaking interiorly in Christian lives, when baptism leads to community and to ethics, then the mutual witness of sacramental and non-sacramental Christians may also be mutually heard. Quakers, Salvationists and some non-baptizing Christian groups in Asia and Africa will need the churches who actually physically do the *ordo* and they will need *ordo*-like catechesis and community-formation, so that their own spirituality does not become gnostic. But the sacramental churches will also need the witness of those for whom the only water is that of the interior speech of the Spirit and the resultant life of self-giving service is "participation in the Body of Christ". Astonishingly, Ignatius and his witness might be a meeting place for both.

Furthermore, when the entire process of the *ordo* is trinitarian, when the triune name is the "shape" of baptism, when faith in God by identification with Jesus Christ leads to the community of the Spirit, then disputes about the "formula" of baptism may not be so church-dividing.[31] Indeed, we may be able to recognize both of the biblical "formulas" as well as baptisms without a formula, if the process of baptizing itself is trinitarian. We may be able to enter more profoundly into the discussion of appropriate and orthodox language to express the mystery of the Trinity in our day, including criticism of the ways in which "Father" and "Son" have been used to express a faith which is not orthodox or Christian.

Further, when participation in the entire *ordo* is participation in the eschatological gift of the Spirit, when passing through the water brings us into the community of the Spirit, we may be able to rejoice in signs of the Spirit added to the rite: laying on of hands, anointing with oil, sealing. But we may also be able to resist either separating these signs from the *ordo*, as if they were themselves a new and separate thing, or castigating those Christians who do not use these signs, resting instead in the Spirit's action through water and the word.

Many other such questions may also be illuminated in our conversation here as we take the re-membering of the *ordo* into consideration. But common work on these questions and common restoration of the *ordo* may indeed help us to let the astonishing, gracious gift of baptism into Jesus Christ stand forth as a word to our time, amid our need, answering our cries.

NOTES

[1] Ignatius, *To the Romans* 7:1b,2b-3; Greek text in Kirsopp Lake, *The Apostolic Fathers*, Vol. 1, Cambridge, Harvard UP, 1959, p.234.

[2] *Ibid.*, 2:1b: "For if you should be silent concerning me, I am word of God. But if you should desire my flesh, I shall again be only a cry"; Greek text in Lake, *op. cit.*, pp.226-28.

[3] *Ibid.*, 6:16, 2b-3a: "I seek that one who died for us; I want that one who rose for us. The time of birth-labour is upon me... Let me receive the pure light; having arrived there, I shall be a full human being. Permit me to be an imitator of the passion of my God"; Greek text in Lake, *op. cit.*, pp.232-34.

[4] Cf. for example, *Martyrdom of Polycarp* 14:2; 15:2.

[5] Ignatius, *op. cit.*, 4:1b: "I am wheat of God, and I am ground by the teeth of the beasts that I might be found pure bread of Christ"; Greek text in Lake, *op. cit.*, p.230.

[6] Cf. Ignatius, *To the Smyrnaeans* 8:2a, where he sees the bishop in the midst of the congregation which is celebrating baptism and then the eucharist: "Wherever the bishop appears, there let the full assembly be, just as wherever Jesus Christ is, there is the catholic church. Without the bishop it is not allowed to baptize nor to hold the meal of love"; Greek text in Lake, *op. cit.*, p.260. This does not imply that the bishop does everything in such a celebration. He *presides*. Cf. *ibid.*, 8:1b: "Let that be considered a reliable thanksgiving at table which is celebrated by the bishop or by the one to whom he turns."

[7] *To the Romans* 7:1. That Ignatius regarded baptism as "arms" for a life-long struggle with evil can be seen in his letter *To Polycarp* 6:2: "Let your baptism abide as arms, faith as helmet, love as spear, patience as armour"; Greek text in Lake, *op. cit.*, p.274.

[8] Ignatius himself characterizes his martyrdom as *becoming a Christian* in truth, as being found to be a Christian – not just being called one; cf. *To the Romans* 3:2.

[9] That Ignatius might have taken his "I" to stand for a whole community of Christians which he believed he carried in himself and represented can be seen in his description of the bishop Polybius, who "came to me in Smyrna, by the will of God and of Jesus Christ, and so rejoiced with me, a prisoner of Christ Jesus, that I beheld the full assembly of you all in him"; *To the Trallians* 1:1b; Greek text in Lake, *op. cit.*, p.212. Cf. *To the Ephesians* 1:3.

[10] *To the Romans* 6:3: "Permit me to be an imitator of the passion of my God. If anyone has him within, let that one understand what I want and sympathize with me, knowing the things which constrain me"; Greek text in Lake, *op. cit.*, p.234.

[11] Dom Gregory Dix, *The Shape of the Liturgy*, Westminster, Dacre, 1945.

[12] For one list, see Gordon Lathrop, "The Lima Liturgy and Beyond", *The Ecumenical Review*, Vol. 48, No. 1, Jan. 1996, p.67, n.17, and in Thomas F. Best and Dagmar Heller, eds, *Eucharistic Worship in Ecumenical Contexts: The Lima Liturgy – and Beyond*, Geneva, WCC Publications, 1998, pp. 22-28.

[13] "Concerning Celebrations of the Eucharist in Ecumenical Contexts: A Proposal from a Group Meeting at Bossey", *The Ecumenical Review*, Vol. 47, No. 3, July 1995, pp.387-91; also published (in English, German and Spanish) in Thomas F. Best and Dagmar Heller, eds, *Eucharistic Worship in Ecumenical Contexts: The Lima Liturgy – and Beyond*, Geneva, WCC, 1998, pp.29ff.

[14] For the report, see Thomas F. Best and Dagmar Heller, eds, *So We Believe, So We Pray: Towards Koinonia in Worship*, Faith and Order Paper No. 171, Geneva, WCC, 1995, pp.4-26, cited hereafter as Ditchingham. For the *ordo* of the eucharist, see Ditchingham paras 4-8, 10, 18, 30, 41, 60.

[15] 1 *Apology* 61-67; Greek text in *PG* 6:420-432; translation in Gordon W. Lathrop, *Holy Things: A Liturgical Theology*, Minneapolis, Fortress, 1993, pp.45,61-64.

[16] See Aidan Kavanagh, *The Shape of Baptism*, New York, Pueblo, 1978, pp.36-37.

[17] Cf. *Didache* 7:2-3: "But if you do not have living water [i.e., running water, river water], baptize in other water, and if you are not able to use cold water then use warm [the reference is probably to public baths]. But if you do not have either, pour out water on the head three times ..."; Greek text in Lake, *op. cit.*, p.320.

[18] Cf. Kavanagh, *op. cit.*, pp.40-42. See also Gabriele Winkler, *Das Armenische Initiationsrituale*, Rome, Oriental Institute, 1979. In its picture of the conversion and reception into Israel of the Egyptian wife of Joseph, the anonymous writing *Asenath* may also give us insight into the patterns of 2nd- and 3rd-century Syrian baptisms.

[19] Indeed, this same pattern, found in Paul and in Peter, could still be used by Christians in their baptismal catechesis. The ancient people of God, the community of royal priests for the world, was formed by being led across the sea to hear the word of God at Sinai and, in the elders, to eat and drink with God (Ex. 24). This ancient people was re-formed by being led across the blossoming desert to hear the word of God, eat together and send food to the poor (Neh. 8). So now in Christ the royal priestly people is formed by being led through the water to word and table and so to witnessing life in the world.

[20] See Gordon W. Lathrop, "The Origin and Early Meanings of Christian Baptism", *Worship*, Vol. 68, No. 6, Nov. 1994, pp.504-22.

[21] See Adela Yarbro Collins, "The Origin of Christian Baptism", in Maxwell E. Johnson, ed., *Living Water, Sealing Spirit: Readings on Christian Initiation*, Collegeville MN, Liturgical Press, 1995, pp.35-57.

[22] On the baptism of Jesus as the primitive model for Christian baptismal theology and practice, see Kilian McDonnell, *The Baptism of Jesus in the Jordan*, Collegeville MN, Liturgical Press, 1996. Ignatius also taught that the baptism of Christ and his passion together made of "the water" a new thing: Jesus Christ "was born and was baptized, that by his passion he might purify the water"; *To the Ephesians* 18:2b; Greek text in Lake, *op. cit.*, p.192.

[23] E. g., *Apostolic Tradition* 21.

[24] Nikos Nissiotis, "The Credible Reception of the Lima Document as the Ecumenical Conversion of the Churches", in Max Thurian, ed., *Churches Respond to BEM*, Vol. 3, Faith and Order Paper No. 135, Geneva, WCC, 1987, p.xi.

[25] On this, see for example *Churches Respond to BEM*, Vol. 1, p.71; Vol. 2, pp.41-28, Vol. 3, p.35.

[26] See, among many other references, *Ibid.*, Vol. 2, pp.126f.

[27] *Ibid.*, Vol. 3, p.149.

[28] *Ibid.*, Vol. 3, pp.149f.; Vol. 6, p.11.

[29] *Ibid.*, Vol. 3, p.16; Vol. 6, p.11.

[30] *Ibid.*, Vol. 3, p.65.

[31] See *Ibid.*, Vol. 2, pp.45, 59, 71, 184, 328.

Walking with the Word

A Response to Gordon Lathrop

PAUL SHEPPY

Gordon Lathrop has invited us in his paper to engage in a journey of re-discovery. For many the path to unity has been a long time walking. There is always the chance that we simply go round in circles – as a parody of "Onward, Christian Soldiers" puts it:

> Like a mighty tortoise
> moves the church of God;
> Brothers [sic], we are treading
> where we've always trod.

Prof. Lathrop proposes a fresh path, which he suggests will avoid old dead-ends, and his paper is a careful map for those who will walk together. I am amazed and delighted to have this opportunity to make a formal response. I am amazed because where there are two Baptists there are usually three opinions, and I am delighted because the journey to which we are invited is such an important and exciting one. However, since it is best in any journeying to be sure about our departure point even if we do not know how or where we will arrive, I ought to register a third emotion beyond amazement and delight. I feel like the man who, when asked for directions to such and such a town, replied: "Well, if I were you, I would not start from here!"

Among British Baptists *Baptism, Eucharist and Ministry* is not an agreed position paper, and it would be less than honest to suggest otherwise. When the WCC invited churches to respond to BEM, British Baptists were unable to make a response which had central policy status. All we could do was to report on congregational practice; and that practice is diverse.

The practice is diverse because the theology is diverse; and the divergence relates to the pilgrimage of faith Gordon Lathrop refers to, on which he sees baptism as the sign of life-long formation in faith. There are two main lines of baptismal ecclesiology among British Baptists, and describing them briefly may help to show why many in my tradition would have difficulties in walking this path. I do not believe that we can ignore the journey which has brought so many frustrations simply to begin another. In Britain the Church of England and the Methodist Church are once again starting to talk of structural unity. They will have to walk a new way, but they cannot pretend that the past has not happened, and part of their journeying will necessitate the task of remembering. Here, among you, I have to remember.

What is baptism?

It is commonly acknowledged that Baptists understand baptism to be the immersion of believers in the name of the Trinity upon profession of faith. That is why we prefer the term "believers' baptism" to "adult baptism".[1] Our insistence on this springs from our understanding of the church as the gathered company of believers. Church membership is thus more than entry on the parish electoral roll; it is ordination to discipleship and mission in community. The local congregation possesses in full measure the promises of God, the presence of Christ and the life of the Spirit. While it cannot live in isolation from Christ's disciples of other times and places, the local congregation exercises the royal priesthood of all believers in the liberty of the children of God, sealed and animated by the Spirit. Of course, we do not all live up to this vision – that is our sin; yet it is our calling – and that is our testimony.

Such an ecclesiological stance leads us to a baptismal policy which sees the baptism of believers as the entrance to the pilgrimage of faith undertaken in the company of Christ's people, the church. For some (no matter what the present faith of the potential church member), if baptism has not been by immersion on profession of faith, then admission to the local congregation is not a possibility. Believers of long standing who were baptized as infants, who have been confirmed and who are living out their Christian faith in love of God, neighbour and enemy are nevertheless required to be baptized. Those who make this demand deny any charge of re-baptism, since they do not understand what occurred previously as being itself baptism. Another group, while having reservations about infant baptism will take the lived faith of other Christians as adequate and require no more than a re-affirmation of baptismal vows.

Both these groups are in one sense wedded to a common understanding of baptism as primarily admission to the church. In that, at least, they have a great deal of church history on their side. At the same time, the "confusion is worse confounded" by the fact that a given baptismal theology and practice do not necessarily imply a correlative eucharistic practice as regards admission to the Lord's supper.[2]

The more inclusive of these views has a further expression, which needs recounting, not least because none of the papers distributed in advance of this consultation refers to perhaps the greatest 20th-century Baptist writer on baptism, George Beasley-Murray. For many years Beasley-Murray has argued that "believers' baptism" ought more properly to be understood as "conversion baptism".[3] This has resulted in two apparently contrary principles. Baptism is correctly and normatively to be linked to conversion, and as such it implies entry to the community of faith, the church. At the same time, while the link with conversion is primary, conversion is a way of daily living in obedience to the risen Lord, and baptism is the initiating sign of such life. This polarity leads Beasley-Murray to conclude that where Christians who were baptized in infancy come for membership of a local Baptist congregation, their baptism cannot now be separated from their conversion and we ought not to demand it.

However, in an article written in 1994, Beasley-Murray moved on further.[4] He challenged those who have waged the traditional argument about baptism to adopt a new strategy. What he suggests is virtually a post-modern stance, though he himself does not use this term. He argues that, since there is divergence of theology and practice resulting from different presuppositions, it will be best simply to adapt to what is the case rather than rehearsing the arguments for what ought to happen. The task then becomes one of accommodating variant theological models and constructs in an endeavour to understand and value rather than assault and deny one another.

Another British Baptist, Morris West, has noted in comprehensive detail how different churches express the relationship between baptism, confirmation, membership and eucharistic observance.[5] West urges close attention both to the ecumenical history of the past forty years and to the peculiar experience of Local Ecumenical Partnerships (LEPs). LEPs are groupings of churches and congregations at the local level authorized and sponsored by regional church leaders. They may share buildings, ministries and congregations or any combination of the three. Alternatively, they may be separate congregations in their own buildings and with their own ministerial oversight who share in a covenanted mission task. LEPs live out the problems of one baptism in two modes: they experience at first hand the disciplines of shared or unshared eucharist, and they confront in themselves the difficulties of joint membership of more than one denominational structure. Here I would go on to recall Karl Rahner's observation that the smallest example of the Christian congregation is Christian marriage. For many such ecclesial communities, ecumenical encounter is felt most painfully where two partners are

Christian communicants in good standing of separate traditions. They are united in the marriage bed, but parted at the foretaste of the bridal feast of the Lamb.

As West rehearses the history, one feels what he describes: "a paradoxical mixture of ecumenical weariness and ecumenical enthusiasm verging on impatience!" Like Beasley-Murray, West has a healthy respect for the theology, but is consumed by the pastoral imperative. He concludes his paper by suggesting that we should approach the issue by means of a theology of the child. Whatever rite we use to welcome the child into the church – baptism, blessing, presentation – it must mark a process of commitment by the church to recover a catechetical pathway to the faith which speaks the name of Jesus as Lord.

Ordo, and "the water that speaks": a call to journey

In his commentary on Isaiah Eusebius of Caesarea draws a contrast between the voice (John the Baptist) which cries "Prepare a way" and the Word of God (Jesus) for whom the way is prepared.[6] Augustine articulates this more explicitly: "John was a voice, but the Lord in the beginning was the Word."[7]

If baptism is to be the water that speaks, there are three voices making utterance: God in Christ reconciling all to himself, the Christian community affirming the apostolic faith, and the individual believer who is claimed by Christ and who joins herself or himself to the community. If one of these voices is missing, the speech of the water is in some sense impaired. And what is the "word" that the water speaks in echo of the voice of God, of the church, of the believer? "Jesus is Lord."

What Gordon Lathrop invites us to consider is baptism as programmatic rather than punctiliar. Two discussion documents published by British Baptists in 1996 indicate that, while not approaching the question from a liturgical perspective, there is a willingness to re-examine the catechetical structures relating to baptism. The first is a study guide in which six Baptist scholars address believers' baptism in systematic rather than New Testament terms. *Reflections on the Water* is a collection of papers designed to initiate a new way into the old debate in much the same way as our meeting here is intended.[8] Baptism is described as evidence of God's sacramental freedom to act, a reminder of the link between the materiality of creation and its redemption, a political act, an act of community within the world and a call to pilgrimage. A response is also offered by Christopher Rowlands, Dean Ireland Professor of New Testament at the University of Oxford, who urges Baptists not to forsake their New Testament theology of baptism and invites further reflection on the place of children and the catechumenate.

The second document, published by the Doctrine and Worship Committee of the Baptist Union of Great Britain, rehearses in more detail the agenda to which I referred earlier: the Baptist difficulties with the relationship of personal faith in the practice of infant baptism and so on.[9] However, the committee has not allowed the old questions to forge the old answers. The document concludes by investigating the catechetical agenda, and thus allows some accommodation of the possibility of less confrontational approaches. This is not an entirely new way of thinking, as I indicated earlier, but it is being given increased impetus as Baptist congregations join LEPs, where baptismal and membership policies have to be very carefully agreed. With some notable exceptions, Baptists have not excelled in the field of liturgy. However, there is a sea-change. In September 1996 the Joint Liturgical Group of Great Britain organized a conference in England on the future of Christian worship in Britain. Delegates attended from the black churches, from the Greek Orthodox, from the Salvation Army as well as from the "historic" traditions of the West. To my astonishment the largest group were Baptists – twenty percent of those present!

Gordon Lathrop's paper may represent an unfamiliar starting-point for many members of my faith and order, and it remains true that there are some who will want the journey to be one-way – rather in the manner of the elderly minister who said, "You worship God in your way. We'll worship him in his." Nevertheless, there is a move among many to find ways in which we can acknowledge the validity of one another's baptism. The image of the journey in which baptism is the programmatic *ordo* is very helpful, and I believe that there are creative possibilities here. Whether all can travel this road, I do not know – indeed, I doubt it – but I am content to try and I am grateful to Gordon Lathrop for this new map. Like all maps it will need revision where we find that the cartographer has diverged from the geographical realities, but that is not an argument against map-making or trail-blazing.

In the Priestly account of the creation the *ruach* of God hovers over the waters of chaos bringing order. In the Exodus the *shekinah* of God leads the people through the Sea of Reeds to salvation from bondage. Baptism is the place of our new creation, the journey from bondage is mapped, the chaos of death is confronted and the order of resurrection assumed. Where baptism is seen as a destination rather than as a point of departure we have got it wrong, whoever we are. The 1995 Church of England report *On the Way*, drafted in large measure by Michael Vasey, echoes this stress on journey and pilgrimage (also found in the Rite of Christian Initiation of Adults), and proposes a catechetical programme.[10] The report proposes four texts which might shape the catechumenate: the

Lord's prayer, the Apostles' Creed, Jesus' summary of the law and the Beatitudes. Although Baptists have been hesitant about creeds, my own view is that these four texts would provide a useful ecumenical core for the task of catechetical instruction before and after baptism.

I look forward to the rest of the conference in the hope that we will have the courage to journey and the wisdom to journey well. Let the water speak: "Jesus is Lord", it will say. In obedience, let us walk in newness of life with the Word made flesh.

NOTES

[1] Of course, many of those who baptize infants want to make the same claim: the infants they baptize are believers. Baptists have difficulty in understanding in what sense infants may be said to believe. In the course of the consultation at Faverges, we agreed that the phrase "those who are able to answer for themselves" better describes what Baptists want to assert.

[2] For example, a church may recognize as a Christian someone who is not baptized by immersion. Such a person may be admitted to the table, but not to the membership of the local congregation. The church is rigorist on baptism but hospitable at the table.

[3] This process found classic expression in G.R. Beasley-Murray, *Baptism in the New Testament*, London, Macmillan, 1964.

[4] G.R. Beasley-Murray, "The Problem of Infant Baptism: An Exercise in Possibilities", in *Festschrift Günter Wagner*, Bern, Peter Lang, 1994.

[5] W.M.S. West, "Christian Initiation and Church Membership: a Report", London, Churches Together in England, 1996.

[6] *Commentary on Isaiah*, ch. 40.

[7] Sermon 293,3.

[8] P.S. Fiddes, ed., *Reflections on the Water: Understanding God and the World through the Baptism of Believers*, Macon GA, Smith & Helwys, 1996.

[9] *Believing and Being Baptized: Baptism, So-called Re-baptism and Children in the Church*, Didcot, Baptist Union of Great Britain, 1996.

[10] *On the Way: Towards an Integrated Approach to Christian Initiation*, London, Church House Publishing, 1995; cf. *Rite of Christian Initiation of Adults*, Chicago, Liturgy Training Publications, 1988.

A. EXPERIENCES FROM THE LIFE OF THE CHURCHES

Black Africa and Baptismal Rites

F. KABASELE LUMBALA

In presenting the experience of African churches in the inculturation of baptismal rites, I will speak about the Latin Catholic churches, which I know best. The rites I shall describe are not yet officially recognized by the universal church: we are in the midst of a process of discernment and the status of new liturgical forms, especially where they are different from the Western tradition, is not always clear.

Despite this, however, the African churches have already taken substantial steps in inculturation, especially with regard to rites. The eucharist, which was already approved in 1988 with compromises on the wording, has only opened the door to other sacraments.

As to baptism, I would like to remind you that the process followed by the church fathers[1] is exactly the one followed by African communities:[2] they try to talk the language of their peoples in the celebrations; they read the lives of their peoples from the gospel perspective and in the light of the Christian message. This is what has given birth to new rituals, symbols and gestures in comparison with the ones proposed by the Second Vatican Council.

In this short presentation, I will describe only two baptismal rites, situating them within African cultures and Christian theology.

Christian initiation of adults

In Africa, the celebrations of Christian initiation as the *ordo* presents them to us raise the problem of intelligibility, a problem of communication. The networks to which black Africa seems to be connected in so far as what is said and done in Christian initiation is concerned recall directly the signs and symbols of its traditional initiations. In what degree can these signs and symbols express the message of Christian initiation, and how can these celebrations echo the lives of the Africans? The trial rituals initiated here and there in black Africa seem to respond to these preoccupations.[3]

Our first illustration comes from the interior of Zaire, more precisely from the South East. The final stage in the Christian initiation of adults is preferably celebrated during Easter Eve, preceded by two other stages: first, the stage during which the catechumens are locked up for a period of asceticism and intense prayer; second, the stage that aims at opening the mind through particular instruction and some practice. On Easter Eve, after the readings and homily, the achievement of the sacrament is celebrated:

- *Proclamation of faith and renunciation of Satan.*
- *Miming death-resurrection:* the candidates are told to lie down on mats; they are covered with banana leaves; a penitence or mourning song is struck up, or simply silence is kept. Then the priest moves forward holding the candidate's right arm. He raises it shouting in a strong voice: "Christ has risen from the tomb, living for ever. You too, live with him, rise." As the candidate is getting up, Psalm 117 (118):16-17 is sung: "The right hand of the Lord has risen, the right hand of the Lord has performed a feat of strength. No, I shall not die, I shall live to tell the Lord's works."
- *Water rite:* Water is poured on the candidate's head while the trinitarian formula is recited, and incense is wafted around the newly baptized.
- *Conferring the new name:* When the priest asks the godfather to tell him the candidate's name, the godfather answers by reciting his godchild's genealogies, at the end of which he pronounces the name chosen for baptism as the "crowning" of his identity. Once the godfather has finished, the priest greets the newly baptized adult in a special way, solemnly pronouncing his new name aloud. He shakes his hand warmly. The name is no longer necessarily a Western Christian name of some saint. It can be chosen in the local culture, provided that it is in connection with God's gift.[4]
- *Godfather's commitment:* The priest invites the godfather to commit himself to his role as guide in the godchild's faith. The godfather then takes hold of a tool of his trade (a hoe for farmers, a book for teachers or office workers, a measuring instrument for traders). He does a dance step or simply walks round his godchild, then comes and takes up position in front of the priest, to whom he holds out the tool. The priest blesses it, informing him that from now onwards all his activities will have to proclaim salvation in Christ.
- *Confirmation ointment:* The priest lays his hands on the baptized person and anoints him on the forehead.
- *Ointment with white kaolin (white clay):* The priest puts some white kaolin on the candidate's arms, cheeks and feet, telling him he is a

new being with new status in the church and wishing him fruitfulness and prosperity in his baptismal commitment. He makes him pass in front of the congregation, saying: "Just as Christ has passed from this world to his Father, in the same way N. has passed from the bondage of sin to liberation, from death to life. What has just been fulfilled to him is what we have to live, all of us who have been baptized. Let us applaud N. and exult with jubilation." A song of joy and a hallelujah are struck up. The offerings are prepared and the eucharist takes place, during which the newly baptized will accede to the table of the Lord.

In our Bantu traditions, initiation is a continuous maturing and begetting process, spread over the whole of life. It consists in dying to oneself and being born again. Lying on the ground or in a hole and then getting up again is a symbol used in several tribal initiations. Another cultural element concerns the name. The name represents the person – hence the whole long ceremony going over the person's genealogy to finish with the Christian name. The godfather's dance around the godchild is a sign of harmonization. From now on the godfather's life (his trade practice included) has to be in harmony (same rhythm) with this baptism, with his godchild's growth in faith.

Baptism of infants

The second example is baptism of infants. The problem posed in the West concerning baptism of infants as not in harmony with the theological understanding of baptism as the sacrament of faith and adhesion to Christ is more or less resolved in Africa by understanding baptism as a rite of harmonization and personal growth, which are able to occur at any age. The sin of Adam and Eve has introduced disharmony into the universe and disturbed creation. Our sin continues to disorient creation and introduce disharmony into it. Consequently, the Bantus willingly and fervently welcome rites that restore harmony in life and in the person. And there are many such rites in Bantu traditions, according to the way in which children are born and the position they have at birth.

Concerning the baptism of infants, St Augustine said that since infants have been injured because of their parents, it is therefore normal that adults present them to the doctor so that they may be cured. With the Bantus, we would say: the adults are the ones who provoke disharmony in the universe through their acts; and since the beings influence one another like communicating vessels, this disharmony strikes the children fatally. That is why baptism, which puts things back in place and reorients them towards God thanks to Christ, restores personal harmony, which is essential for our children's personal completeness.

Here is a ritual during a eucharistic celebration, after the readings and the homily:

- *Welcoming:* The priest and parents make the sign of the cross on the child.
- *Name rite:* To the question as to what name they have given to the child, the parents answer by reciting the family tree, at the end of which they pronounce the Christian name, as if to indicate that baptism is a matter of new personal fulfilment, a new stage of growing of the same individual. So the child does not leave its family at baptism, but the latter marks a decisive stage in its personal completeness. Beneath this we can discern an African soteriology and ecclesiology: "As a baptized African, I do not move from my village by entering the church, but the church becomes the place where my village acquires new dimensions." Salvation in Christ makes me reach my personal completeness: Jesus is the source and the end of my being.
- *Prayers of the faithful.*
- *Blessing of the water.*
- *Laying on of hands,* with prayer of exorcism and calling on the Holy Spirit.
- *Renunciation of Satan and profession of faith.*
- *Baptismal bath.*
- *Royal ointment,* with words indicating that the baptized child has become another Christ, priest, king and pastor.
- *The godfather's commitment:* The same gestures are made as for the rite of adults – dancing or walking round his godchild, holding out the instruments of his trade for the blessing.
- *Anointing with white kaolin:* The same gestures and formulas as for the rite of adults, to symbolize a desire for growth and radiance of the new life. It should be noted that this white kaolin rite has replaced the lit candle and the white garment. This colour is most meaningful in our Bantu traditions. Here it evokes the crossing of a vital threshold, a personal maturity, as well as assuming a role in society. That is why it is given to the newly initiated, the newborn children during the rites of restoring harmony. It is also given to chiefs who make an official sortie to exercise their duties. All these meanings totally cover the symbolism of the lit candle and the white garment of the official ritual.

Conclusion

The rite and the human person are closely bound: a rite cannot be imported from one culture to another without negotiation and re-arrangements. That is what happened during the first centuries of the church in the West and the East. That is what is happening in Africa today. The message of baptism remains the same as the one emerging from the New Testament;[5] for if local signs are used, it is to proclaim not the local culture but salvation in Jesus Christ. This message, however, is transmitted in different ways, with local signs and symbols, which may lead to other theological accents, for it is the incarnation process that calls for it; it is the truth of language that requires it; it is even faithfulness to Christ's message that postulates it.

A message that is not translated into a nation's cultural fabric is not transmitted, and we would then be unfaithful to the very nature of Christianity, religion of the incarnated Word.

NOTES

[1] See the excellent article by A.J. Chupungco, "Baptism in the Early Church and its Cultural Settings", in S. Anita Stauffer, ed., *Worship and Culture in Dialogue*, Geneva, Lutheran World Federation, Department of Studies, 1994, pp.39-56.

[2] See *Devenir chrétien en Afrique* (Becoming a Christian in Africa), Koumi encounter, 1972. See also *Dilila bimany lou bya lupandu* (Ritual of the Diocese of Mbujimay), Kinshasa, 1996, and my book *Symbolique bantu et symbolique chrétienne* (Bantu Symbolism and Christian Symbolism), Kinshasa, Faculté catholique de Kinshasa, 1991.

[3] See *Devenir chrétien en Afrique*, Koumi encounter, Bobo Dioulasso, 1977; *Pâques africaines aujourd'hui* (African Easter Today), Paris, 1989.

[4] Arrangement made by the episcopate of Zaire after the suppression of Western Christian names by the regime of Mobuto Sese Seko in the interest of the policy of authenticity; see *Eglise au service de la nation zaïroise* (Church in the Service of the Zairean Nation), Brussels, 1972, p.210.

[5] See the good summary by Gordon W. Lathrop, "Baptism in the New Testament and its Cultural Settings", in *Worship and Culture in Dialogue*, p.35.

Baptism and Confirmation in the Church of South India

JOHN W. GLADSTONE

Baptism and eucharist are the two sacraments accepted in the Church of South India (CSI). However, confirmation is necessary to take part in the eucharist. The order of service for confirmation is called "Order of Service for the Reception of Baptized Persons into the Full Membership of the Church, commonly called Confirmation".[1] The title itself denotes that confirmation has no independent position without baptism. It is the affirmation of the gift of the Holy Spirit by which the candidate is assured of God's love, being God's child until the day of redemption, and is empowered for a godly life in this world. At the same time by confirmation a candidate is received into the full fellowship of the church. The candidate also accepts Jesus Christ as his or her personal saviour.

In 1954 Canon W. Elphick observed:

> The CSI confirmation service seems to us to be much more effective than any Anglican rite because it makes clear to the candidates what are their main duties as grown-up members of the church, both lets candidates hear read the accounts of the Laying-on of Hands recorded in the Acts and has a welcome, at the end of the service, of the candidates on the part of the congregation to make them realize that they really are expected to share in the grown-up-life and duties of the congregation. At the same time the central acts of prayer for the coming of the Holy Spirit and the Laying-on of Hands are as strongly emphasized as they are in the Anglican rite.[2]

As early as 1923, at the Pasumalai negotiations for the formation of the CSI, confirmation was a matter of discussion. One commentator feared an effort "of relegate what the apostolic church regarded as a necessary element in baptism, as the special symbol and effectual sign of the gift of the Holy Ghost, to the permanent inferiority of a rite which 'may be administered... in any congregation which desires it'".[3] Against this, confirmation was seen as a rite which naturally follows baptism, and through which the church believes that a special gift of the Holy Spirit is bestowed. Confirmation was one of the areas where consensus was arrived at among the negotiating churches which later became CSI.

In the CSI order of service for baptism of infants the following question is asked of the parents: "Will you encourage him/her later to be received into the full fellowship of the church by confirmation; so that, established in faith by the Holy Spirit, he/she may partake of the Lord's supper and go forth into the world to serve God faithfully in his church?" The answer is, "We will, God being our helper."[4] Thus on the occasion of infant baptism the CSI liturgy affirms that baptism should be followed by confirmation.

In the order of service for confirmation the minister says:

> In your baptism you were received into the fellowship of Christ and sealed as members of the family and household of God. Now you come, of your own choice, to ratify the solemn covenant then made, to profess your faith in the Lord Jesus, to consecrate yourselves to him, and to receive the gifts which he is waiting to bestow.[5]

In the case of believers' baptism (baptism of adults), after the baptism the minister exhorts: "and encourage them to attend diligently to right instruction in God's holy word, and so to prepare themselves for confirmation, that, being established in faith by the Holy Spirit, they may come with due preparation to receive the Lord's supper".[6]

The teaching and practice of the CSI is that confirmation is the continuation of the "mystical" aspect of holy baptism. Both baptism and confirmation are acts of the Holy Spirit. Therefore they are not two different sacraments. In the prayer of confirmation the minister says: "Almighty God, our heavenly Father, who by holy baptism hast received these thy children into thy family: Establish them in faith, we beseech thee, by the Holy Spirit, and daily increase in them thy manifold gifts of grace."[7] It is thus affirmed that confirmation is continuation of the sacrament of baptism. Confirmation provides an opportunity to everyone to grow in faith and to affirm it publicly.

Behind the practice of confirmation is the intention to take seriously 1 Corinthians 2:28: "Examine yourselves, and only then eat of the bread and drink of the cup." The CSI affirms the need for every believer to be prepared to receive the "holy mysteries". Acts 9:17-18 has also influenced the practice of confirmation in the CSI. Thus confirmation is done by "laying on of hands". The minister lays his hands on the head of the candidate and prays as follows:

> Strengthen, O Lord, this thy child with thy heavenly grace, that he/she may continue thine for ever, and daily increase in thy Holy Spirit, until he/she come unto thine everlasting kingdom.[8]

Also the concluding prayer says:

> Let the Holy Spirit ever be with them; and so lead them in the knowledge and obedience of thy word.[9]

The CSI order of service for confirmation has three parts: (1) affirmation of faith, including the open proclamation that the candidate affirms Jesus Christ as his/her personal saviour and also the saviour of the world; (2) prayer with laying-on of hands; (3) acceptance into the full membership and fellowship of the church, for which we depend on the working of the Holy Spirit.

Confirmation makes the teaching ministry of the church important. Baptized members of the church are given instruction in the Christian faith. In the CSI all confirmed members are called to a fresh awareness about this role in life as participants in the body and blood of Christ. They are called to understand that:

1. Personal faith and commitment to Christ are essential to continue within the "body of Christ". Everyone is incorporated into the "body of Christ" at the time of baptism, but the fullness and continuity depend upon life with Christ. This demands the acceptance of Jesus Christ as Lord and saviour personally. At the same time, the candidate is helped to see Jesus as the saviour of the world. One of the questions asked in the CSI order of service is: "Do you accept the Lord Jesus Christ as your personal saviour and the saviour of the world?" The faith of the church becomes the faith of each individual member. Corporate affirmation becomes personal acceptance.
2. A person who is confirmed is not a mere spectator in the church and in the world. He or she is a disciple of Christ. There were many people who heard of Jesus; but only a few were accepted into the discipleship. The person who is confirmed has all the responsibilities of a disciple of Jesus Christ. Thus the minister asks: "Do you acknowledge yourself bound to confess the faith of Christ crucified and risen, and to continue as his faithful servant unto your life's end, bearing witness to him both in word and in deed?"[10] The person is assured of full membership and participation in the life of the church.
3. A person becomes a full member of the church. As an expression of this privilege the member receives the body and blood of Christ. At confirmation the candidate promises to participate in the Lord's supper in fellowship with other Christians.

So, according to the practice in the CSI, confirmation is a very solemn occasion which completes what has begun at baptism and leads to new discipleship. In the history of liturgy this combines the practices which existed in different traditions which joined together in CSI.

NOTES

[1] In *The Church of South India: The Book of Common Worship, As Authorized by the Synod 1962*, London, New York, Madras, Oxford UP, 1963, pp.123-30.
[2] W. Elphick, "Bangalore Brotherhood of St Peter and the CSI", *Theology*, Vol. 57, 1954, p.260.
[3] For the discussion and notes, see in Bengt Sundkler, *Church of South India: The Movement towards Union 1900-1947*, London, Lutterworth, 1954, pp.150-51.
[4] "Holy Baptism II: The Baptism of Infants", in *The Church of South India: The Book of Common Worship*, p.118.
[5] *Ibid.*
[6] "Holy Baptism I: The Baptism of Persons Able to Answer for Themselves", *ibid.,* pp.111-12.
[7] *Ibid.*, p.128.
[8] *Ibid.*, pp.128f.
[9] *Ibid.*, p.129.
[10] *Ibid.*, p.127.

Baptism in Asia and its Cultural Settings

The Reformed Experience in Korea

CHANGBOK CHUNG

The discussion of the inculturation of the liturgy is a rather recent development in the Protestant churches of Korea, for reasons which will become clear as I proceed. But before I begin my reflections, I must indicate the limits of how I shall address this topic. I cannot possibly speak about the entirety of Asia, nor do I dare speak for all the churches in Asia, particularly the Roman Catholic Church, since ecumenical conversation in my own country is still in a very early stage. But as a Korean and as a Calvinist I will speak about the cultural context of Buddhism, Confucianism and Shamanism as they have formed the cultures of China, Japan and Korea.

I must also underscore that I represent a unique form of the Calvinist family of churches. Presbyterianism is without question the dominant form of Protestantism in Korea. Its origins go back only to 1884, when the first Presbyterian and Methodist missionaries arrived. It has been observed that the dominance of the Calvinist religion in Korea may well have to do with its striking similarity to Confucianism in terms of respect for intellectualism, discipline and ethical seriousness.

Moreover, it must be acknowledged that the phenomenon of a Calvinist missionary church is unusual. Karl Barth has remarked on the singular lack of interest in mission on the part of the 16th-century churches of the Reformation. And, of course, in the case of Calvinist churches one must take into account the effect on mission of the theological emphasis on the doctrine of election. This was precisely the issue that convulsed North American Calvinism at the time of the Great Awakening and the preaching of Jonathan Edwards. So the early Presbyterian missionaries, deeply influenced by the scholasticism of Princeton, were also unusual in that they were necessarily committed to an evangelistic approach to their vocation. This must be born in mind when considering cultural adaptation – or its absence. In a word, Korea was neither Geneva, nor Edinburgh, nor Westminster, nor Philadelphia, nor Princeton! Further, there were in Korea other religions which, as Father Chupungco puts it, had to be dealt with not only by "silent reproach", but more seriously by "denunciation or protest".[1]

"Reinterpretation" probably did not strike those early Presbyterians as a feasible option, not only because the existing Roman Catholic mission had already taken up some of that agenda, but also, more importantly, because 19th-century Presbyterians had very little cultic tradition which might have enabled them to manage such an option. Remember that the first attempt at a liturgical book in US Presbyterianism was the 1905 Book of Common Worship, two full decades after the initial Korean mission. And Methodism was in very much the same situation, having in 1784 adopted, but then forgotten, Wesley's adaptation of the Anglican Book of Common Prayer. Thus, even though, as Prof. Lathrop affirms, "Christian liturgy can itself be regarded as an instance of 'culture'",[2] the early Reformed missionaries found themselves confronting powerful "cultures" with none of their own, except Calvinistic scholasticism and an evangelistic message based on the Bible.

The sacramental life and consciousness of 19th-century US Presbyterianism was minimal. Initiatory rites were limited to the baptism of the infants of believers (which has never become the accepted norm in Korean Presbyterianism), the catechetical rhythms of Sunday school and preparation for admission to church membership, with absolutely no trace of a sacramental rite such as confirmation. Further, this Presbyterianism knew nothing of the classic Christian calendar, which might have provided a "counter-culture" to that of the prevailing religions. The only annual festival these missionaries brought with them to Korea was not Christmas, Easter or Pentecost, but the US Thanksgiving festival, which remains to this day the virtually central annual festival of the churches (celebrated on the third Sunday of November). And this is in spite of the fact that Koreans have a traditional harvest feast (*Chusook*) – which obviously had to be rejected because its ceremonies involved the veneration of ancestors at their grave-sites.

Response – and reaction

Thus Protestant Christianity came to Korea as a mix of evangelistic and prophetic impulses which had to resist any compromise with native beliefs and social customs. As in many centuries and lands, this need met a counter-force in persecution. In Korea it came with the near-half century of Japanese occupation, which sought to undermine not only Christianity but also much of native Korean history and culture. Under such circumstances the question of "inculturation" becomes both complex and challenging, if not fearful in its consequences for faith and life. And under such circumstances the sacramental life of the church was very difficult to define. Out of pastoral necessity, the Lord's supper was a rare occurrence, and baptism was administered only after a lengthy time of training and preparation of believing candidates, thus shifting the focus of the rite from incorporation (as with infants) to conversion (as with believers). This effectively broke the essential link between the two sacraments (and with the essential reality of the church as community) so well expressed by the Reformed scholar Ronald S. Wallace: "Baptism mainly bears witness to our initiation into this union [with Christ], while the Lord's supper is a sign of our continuation in this union".[3]

In this ecclesial and theological context, what is a Reformed or Calvinist church to make of baptism? And what cultural forms or meanings might be introduced into its practice which speak the cultural "language" while not compromising the Christian character of baptism? As many of our churches now realize, the unquestioned and universal practice of the baptism of the infant children of believers has subjected the sacrament to much misuse and misunderstanding, so that the rite has become a sign of what Dietrich Bonhoeffer called "cheap grace" and, because of its relationship to infants, an unfortunate ritual of "naming" or "christening", devoid of commitment or faith. The role of the "witnessing" parents and church congregation has given way to empty answers to formal, ritual questions. The newly-published Rites for the Christian Initiation of Adults in the Roman Catholic Church and many forms for the baptism of adult believers all testify to this trend in sacramental theology. This of course only reminds us of the early intent and forms of the rite as found in the first few centuries of the church, well attested in Father Chupungco's article.[4] The early churches found it important to use the rite as a clear separation of the baptizand from the prevailing culture, but also to make that separation clear by the use of contemporary forms which were already understood by the baptizands. The same need arose for churches in Asian contexts, but virtually none of that ancient liturgical language was available or acceptable to our early missioners. What were they to do?

For the first time in the Calvinist family of churches, baptism had to be related clearly and consciously to the experience of conversion. The congregation with its officers, lay and ordained, and its discipline of attendance at worship, stewardship and evangelistic mission became the "content" of the baptismal promises, in contrast to the "received rite", in which promises were made by parents concerning the "nurture and admonition of the Lord" for their infant children. "Conversion" had to do very concretely with turning away from the old religions (and often parents), just as Cyril of Jerusalem had to remind his baptizands that their turning from west to east had solemn significance. It is thus of some interest that Korean churches have historically faced the same theological questions which now preoccupy many other churches, including the Roman Catholic Church as it considers the implications of the Rite for the Christian Initiation of Adults. But in a Presbyterianism virtually devoid of a liturgical tradition the emphasis had to fall on catechesis, personal witnessing and the discipline of attendance at worship. Of course, their experience of worship continued to be more evangelistically focused, rather than (in the tradition of Cyril) mystagogically. Inevitably, this led to a much more individualistic sort of piety in contrast to a more corporate, "liturgical" model.

The Asian context

The cultural problem at this point has to do with a central fact in the Asian religious experience – family solidarity over many generations. The inter-generational family formed what in many ways was the corporate and liturgical context for birth, coming of age, respect for authority and commitment to the care of the elderly. In both Buddhism and Confucianism these realities were built into the growth and training of the young, but the particular aspect of the veneration of the deceased (in the context of a Protestantism which had very little feeling for the "communion of the saints") posed a problem which, in Presbyterianism at least, has only been partially and not altogether satisfactorily addressed by the office in the local congregation of lay "elders", who hold a role which is both authoritative and liturgical.

Until quite recently, this office has been open only to males, which has limited the effectiveness of its familial symbolism. In Korean churches in the USA, where the admittance of women to all the offices in the church is now the norm, this is still a problematic issue. Thus, I would suggest, the ways in which the early, patristic church took over both Jewish and Graeco-Roman models for initiation into the church as the Christ-formed family were not available in the Korean context. This problem has more recently been addressed by the use of a "confirmation" rite for those baptized in infancy, functioning in much the same way as the baptism of believers, with emphasis on commitment to witnessing, stewardship and attendance at worship.

This development – surprising enough in a church whose theological ancestor John Calvin denounced confirmation in no uncertain terms[5] – implies that we need to think more carefully about the theology implicit in baptizing infants – just as Karl Barth did in Volume IV, Part 4, of his *Church Dogmatics*, and just as John Calvin did not, obviously in the context of his need to avoid the "errors" of Anabaptist "enthusiasm".

It is at this point that the agenda of "inculturation" comes to mind. Asian cultures and religions have both ritual forms and "theologies" for such incorporation of young children ("believers" into a "family"). So also does the ancient Christian ritual system, with its "sign language" and "sponsorship" of catechumens. The issue is simply whether the traditional cultural pattern of filial piety, with its associated "virtues" with regard to brothers and sisters, husbands and wives, and "neighbours", can be shifted into Christian nurture of children and catechumens by way of reference to Christ as Lord and God as Father?

If such cultural patterns are to be employed with regard both to infants and maturing young people, it will be doubly important that the basic baptismal form of water washing and trinitarian formula be retained. Here, too, our Presbyterian custom of "sprinkling" is woefully inadequate. Either pouring water or in some way entering a pool or stream are quite essential for any use of the sacrament, precisely in order to affirm the uniquely Christian character of the rite. Further, the use of both the trinitarian formula and the biblical reference to the baptism of Jesus in the Jordan needs to be pre-eminent, just as the World Council of Churches' document on *Baptism, Eucharist and Ministry* affirms. It will also be important that the form of the baptismal rite be more inclusive of congregational participation, so as to counter the problematic cultural elements of such rites. This is being suggested in many of the renewed rites of many churches, by performing the rite with sufficient water, in full view of the whole congregation, and often in conjunction with a rite of renewal for the entire congregation. This latter practice, if done at the Easter Vigil, or at seasonally significant times for the baptism of infants, might well be the liturgical "key" that "unlocks" the mystery of the baptism of infants. The timing of such a rite might well be related to the baptism of new believers.

In conclusion, I seek the considerable wisdom of this assembly of scholars from all over the world to assist my church – and others in Korea and throughout Asia – to find a way both to recover the church's own "culture" of worship and to renew in ways that are explicitly Christian the cultural forms and customs which our people know and revere. The historic divisions of Christianity and resulting limitations of liturgical practice and theology have been very unhelpful and even destructive of our cherished tradition of *semper reformanda.* I conclude this appeal by citing the words of the Second Vatican Council:

> The church has existed through the centuries in varying circumstances and has utilized the resources of different cultures in its preaching to spread and explain the message of Christ, to examine and understand it more deeply and to express it more perfectly in the liturgy and in various aspects of the life of

the faithful... The church... can enter into communion with different forms of culture, merely enriching both itself and the cultures themselves.[6]

NOTES

[1] Anscar J. Chupungco, "Baptism in the Early Church and its Cultural Settings", in S. Anita Stauffer, ed., *Worship and Culture in Dialogue*, Geneva, Lutheran World Federation, Department of Studies, 1994, p.41.
[2] Gordon W. Lathrop, "Baptism in the New Testament and its Cultural Settings", in *ibid.*, p.17.
[3] R.S. Wallace, *Calvin's Doctrine of the Word and Sacrament*, Grand Rapids, Eerdmans, 1957, p.150.
[4] *Loc. cit.*, pp.39-56.
[5] Cf. *Institutes of the Christian Religion*, IV.4.4-13.
[6] Pastoral Constitution on the Church in the Modern World (*Gaudium et Spes*), para. 58.

A. EXPERIENCES FROM THE LIFE OF THE CHURCHES

Baptism in Latin America and its Cultural Settings

JACI MARASCHIN

The concept of culture at the end of the 20th century cannot be the same as that of the early church as found in Palestine, Rome and in the East. Christian rites developed in relationship to very definite and clear forms of symbolic dimension. As the church was in the making, the character of that relationship was to some extent original and seminal.

The church itself became a "culture" after Constantine, with the assimilation of some pagan elements which were "Christianized" for the sake of mission. Baptism and eucharist, as the chief symbolic and sacramental elements of the expression of the faith, developed from the preaching of the gospel to different cultures. This development sprang from dialogue, interpretation and accommodation. The church reflected the mediaeval world through two symbolic systems, the Western and the Eastern.

The Western type of ecclesiology was brought to the so-called New World without any criticism or adaptation in the 16th century. Columbus and Cabral were navigators at the service of their kings and lords. Finding America was for them like discovering a paradise: a "nobody's land". Imagine what it was to arrive on those shores which had never been dreamed of by Europeans or by anybody else. They came with their priests and their blessings. They brought with them the "culture of the church" – and why not plant in the new land the chief of their symbols, the cross, just as the astronauts would do with the US flag centuries later when setting foot for the first time on the moon? In the following decades and centuries they ignored the existing cultural symbols and worked to impose their own culture.

And they succeeded. If you visit Latin America, from Mexico to Patagonia, you will notice the remains of a dead past. You will certainly have mixed feelings as to how we Europeans could have devastated the land in such a terrible way. They were Aztecs, Aymaras, Tupis, Incas and Guaranis among many others. They had built amazing civilizations, and their symbols are still kept in museums and stones. But we have destroyed their cultures.

Now we ask, what has happened to native cultures in Latin America? What is the meaning of "Latin America"? It is certainly a melting pot. The few who remain of the original inhabitants of the land are powerless and landless. Black people were brought from Africa as slaves. Then, the Europeans came: Portuguese, Spaniards, Italians, Germans, Polish, Dutch and so on; more recently, Asians, especially from Japan and Korea. Why have they all been attracted to this place? The first conquerors thought that the natives, who seemed to them lazy and immoral, could be transformed into valuable manpower for the sake of profit. The same happened with the African slaves who, since being captured in Africa, led until recent times a life of suffering and abomination. The church they represented was not interested in sensing cultural elements present in the new land. Baptism and eucharist were considered formal truths to be imposed on the local inhabitants for the sake of their souls.

Immigrants tend to keep their own original traditions and symbols. Spanish and Italian people hold strongly to their own form of Catholicism; Japanese have their Buddhas; Germans still venerate Martin Luther. Why should Latin American Calvinists forget Calvin, or Latin American Anglicans their beloved Book of Common Prayer? All this, of course, is very much related to the alien culture which they hold onto as a kind of remembrance.

What is baptism in Latin America? It is what immigrants think it is. Native peoples do not baptize, though they may live by rivers or by the sea. The type of Catholicism brought to Latin America was very superstitious and untheological. This of course has given to baptism a medicinal feature. Among the poor, every child has to be baptized to get rid of diseases and evil spirits. Baptists brought their original practices, and in Latin America they baptize in rivers or by the sea. Like every other continent, Latin America is surrounded by water, but very little attention has been given to this fact in relationship to baptism.

In spite of this context, many Latin Americans are concerned with inculturation in liturgical practice. Our cultural experience is ambiguous and complex. Culture for us is much more than "the symbolic-expressive dimension of social life".[1] There is not in Latin America *a* social life, but diverse types and levels of social life. Should I say "classes"? This is marked by ideological struggles for identity and justice. The presentation of the 46th session of the WCC's Graduate School of Ecumenical Studies in Bossey includes a reminder that applies vividly to our situation. It recognizes:

> the establishment of a global culture, due in part to the forces of modern technology, mass media and the market economy. Giving the illusion of uniting people across national and cultural barriers, it in fact denies the identity of particular cultures and destroys their values when they seem to stand in the way of its logic of capital, know-how and power. Therefore the very nature of culture is questioned as ambivalent. On the one hand it holds a community together by providing people with a common framework of meaning and orientation in life. On the other it contains elements that enslave and degrade.[2]

Culture for us is much more than "the symbolic-expressive dimension of social life". It is also that which has no chance of *being* expressed and, therefore, remains silent, invisible, but latent in the many levels of society as a kind of want, desire or, perhaps, nothing. This is very similar to what some of my psycho-analyst friends would call the "untold" in the narrative of a dream. It is that which is not expressed but only felt.

How can we baptize in such a setting? Christian churches (Roman Catholic, Protestant and Orthodox) follow the official books of their mother churches, be they the Vatican, Geneva, Leipzig, Atlanta, Canterbury or whatever... The inculturation which happened earlier remains the same today. How can this "void" bring some elements to the liturgical celebrations?

The "void" is still there in the refusal in many churches to sing as Latin Americans sing, to dance their dances, to use the colours of their dresses and of their local feasts. The diverse levels of the official culture do not like their "noises".

NOTES

[1] The definition adopted by Gordon W. Lathrop in his essay "Baptism in the New Testament and its Cultural Settings", in S. Anita Stauffer, ed., *Worship and Culture in Dialogue*, Geneva, Lutheran World Federation, Department for Theology and Studies, 1994, pp.17-38.

[2] Programme leaflet published by the Ecumenical Institute, Bossey, 1996.

Criteria for the Inculturation of Baptism

ANSCAR J. CHUPUNGCO

Diversity in unity is a fitting description of what inculturation aims to achieve. Normally we would speak of unity in diversity, but inculturation works the other way around. Because it is premised on unity, inculturation does not bring about division. However, it does confer on unity a variety of expressions. In other words, the diversity produced by inculturation does not, and should not, impinge on unity.

This paper addresses in two parts the question of diversity in unity. The first part deals with the effect of inculturation on the shape of Christian baptism. Inculturation diversifies. The second part offers criteria for preserving the unity of churches as they set out to integrate elements of local culture into the rite of baptism. Inculturation is grafted on unity.

Implications of inculturation

1. For Christian worship in general

As the church stepped out of the Jewish world and entered into contact with the civilization of the Graeco-Roman empire, its Jewish form of worship gradually but steadily gathered new elements drawn from the culture of its converts. The process was dictated by the need to make the liturgy comprehensible to the converts and closer to their experience. From the start the Christian liturgy aimed to be intelligible by its noble simplicity and the use of contemporary language, gestures and symbols.

For example, it neatly distinguished itself from the current mystery rites which were veiled in ceremonies and formularies that often eluded the understanding of neophytes. Besides this, however, the liturgy possesses an inner dynamism that drives it to dialogue with culture. Like the gospel it preaches and celebrates, the liturgy seeks to be grafted in culture.

Dialogue can of course result in a counter-cultural and belligerent stance. But the history of Christian worship assures us that dialogue can also lead to integration and enrichment or, in short, to inculturation.

The integration of local culture into Christian worship was to a large extent responsible for the variety of liturgical shapes which gave rise, from as early as the 3rd century, to the liturgical families in East and West. In most cases these families eventually developed into the phenomenon we commonly call today "particular churches" or "communions of churches". Although doctrinal and political factors also contributed to the development of worship, culture had much to do with the shaping of the Antiochene and Alexandrian families in the East as well as the Roman and other liturgies in the West. It is useful to note that the churches in East and West, even if divided in doctrinal and political persuasion, have continued over the centuries to share with one another their anaphoras and liturgical disciplines. In other words, the process of inculturation which diversified the shape of the liturgy did not produce in its wake a total segregation of churches.

2. For the rite of baptism in particular

This brings us to the question of baptism. Today there is a renewed interest among churches in various parts of the world in integrating local rites of initiation into the shape of Christian baptism. At this point it might be helpful to define terms that are at play in this discussion.

"Shape" refers to the outward form of the rite, which consists of the structure or plan of the celebration, of formularies like the prayer texts and readings, of actions such as immersion, hand-laying and anointing, and of the material elements of water, oil, garment and candle. The traditional name which liturgical documents use for shape is *ordo*.

The shape of baptism has not always been as developed as we know it today. In the New Testament the description of the rite of baptism is confined to the bare essentials, which we may regard as the core. Ephesians 5:26 simply speaks of "washing of water with the word", that is, of a rite made up of an action (washing), a material thing (water) and a formulary (word). Romans 6:4 ("when we were baptized we went into the tomb with him") and Acts 8:38 ("Philip and the eunuch went down into the water") allude to washing by immersion, although there are instances in the New Testament where we can conjecture another mode of washing. On the other hand, Matthew 28:19 specifies that the word is trinitarian, that is, "in the name of the Father, and of the Son, and of the Holy Spirit".

Through contact with different cultures the church gathered elements that developed the core or original shape of baptism. We may say that these later additions explicitly explained and ritually elaborated the apostolic "washing of water with the word". Thus while inculturation enriched the shape through integration of cultural elements, it did not eliminate but rather enhanced what was essential.

Descriptions of the rite of baptism in the 3rd and 4th centuries already include the following: (1) a catechumenate of at least three years, consisting of moral and doctrinal instructions, prayers and exorcisms; (2) a rather intricate liturgical celebration made up of one pre-baptismal and two post-baptismal anointings, renunciation of Satan and commitment to Christ as the candidate turned towards west and east, prayer over the baptismal water, immersion accompanied by the triple profession of faith or credal formula, vesting in white robes, handing of a lighted candle, in Milan the practice of washing the feet of the newly baptized, and in some churches the cup of milk and honey offered to the neophyte at the eucharistic communion; (3) for eight consecutive days after baptism a mystagogical instruction normally given by the bishop to neophytes in their white robes. To this list of ritual elements we add some linguistic items that the church borrowed from mystery rites (*photismos, mystagogia, initiatio*) and from current lexicon (*eiuratio, sacramenti testatio, signaculum fidei, susceptio*). These additives, each in its way, adorned the original "washing in water with the word", in order to bring forth the meaning of the rite.

Not all of the foregoing ritual elaborations survived the test of time. As pastoral needs arose and cultural climates changed, some of them were discarded, to the point that the only elements considered necessary – and this is still the case with emergency baptisms – were washing with water and the word, in short, the original core of the rite of baptism. Still it is good to remember that it has not been the tradition of the church over the past twenty centuries to reduce the liturgy to the essentials of New Testament times. The development of the *ordo* of baptism in the course of time and in different cultural areas is sufficient indication that in matters of ritual we humans need more than the mere essentials: that while the core of the Christian *ordo* must be preserved faithfully, it often requires cultural elaboration in order to be fully understood.

Another term to be clarified is "integration", which is the heart of inculturation. We may define integration as harmonious assimilation. This means that linguistic elements, gestures, symbols and material things which are related to the initiatory practices of a cultural group are introduced into the rite of baptism. With this they interact and dialogue, in order to test whether there is something in their nature which incorrigibly contradicts the teaching of the gospel and whether they are suitable expressions of Christian baptism. If the result is favourable, they are combined with the rite of baptism in order to form an orderly, congruous and culturally enriched *ordo*. Integration can come about in two ways, either by adding new elements to the rite or by re-expressing actual elements of the rite through the method called dynamic equivalence.

Lastly, we need to review the cultural components that interact, dialogue and combine with the baptismal *ordo*. These are values, patterns and institutions that form part of the system of initiation in a particular society. Some of the *values* related to initiation are loyalty to clan or society, responsibility for its well-being and growth, and respect for its tradition. *Patterns*, on the other hand, refer to the typical expressions the group uses for initiation. The answer to the question of how things are typically said and done is a good gauge to determine cultural patterns. For example, how are initiates addressed in words and gestures? How are they welcomed by the community? Finally *institutions* are ritual practices established by tradition. They include not only the elements of the rite, but also persons and roles, time and place, and festivals that might accompany initiation.

Having discussed what is involved when a local congregation inculturates the rite of baptism, we now ask what are the implications of baptismal inculturation for the unity of the church.

History tells us that inculturation brings about diversity in the shape of the liturgy. One implication is that congregations belonging to the same communion will celebrate baptism differently from the received or typical practice of their communion. It can happen, for example, that Roman Catholic congregations in Zaire – or Brazil, or Korea – will adopt a form of baptismal rite that has perhaps radically modified the "typical edition" issued by the head office in Rome. Within the same communion, notable differences will thus emerge in local practice because of differences in culture. The question is whether cultural variations impair the unity of churches.

There is another implication for the unity of the church. It may well happen that congregations belonging to different communions but living in the same cultural milieu will adopt from their locality elements which they hold in common. In the process, because of the integration of native culture, they will adopt a similar, perhaps even identical, shape of baptism. For example, we can envisage a situation in which Anglicans, Presbyterians, Roman Catholics and Lutherans develop baptismal rites that are similar to each other in shape, because their respective congregations live in the same locality and share the same cultural traditions. Evidently, this presupposes that the local congregations are not hostile to their own culture and are supportive of dialogue between Christian worship and culture.

In other words, while inculturation creates diversity within the same communion whose member churches are spread throughout the world, it fosters unity among various local congregations regardless of their ecclesial affiliations. The reason is because inculturation is localization.

Its chief concern is to localize what a congregation has received from the outside source. It levels local differences on account of culture, but it accentuates the distance, again on account of culture, between the local congregation and the communion to which it belongs.

In saying this we should not overlook the basic baptismal unity of all Christian churches: they all acknowledge one baptism for the remission of sins and they all baptize in water in the name of the Blessed Trinity. This is the core of baptism that binds all who profess faith in Jesus Christ. However, this type of unity does not bar diversity in the way we culturally or locally give shape to our common baptism. We should add that neither does diversity encourage the inroads of division among churches, provided of course that inculturation operates within the parameters of unity.

Criteria for inculturation

The framework for inculturation is diversity in unity. As long as cultures differ from each other, inculturation will foster diversity in the celebration of the baptismal *ordo*. We have discussed above the implications of diversity. The question facing us now is how churches can keep baptismal unity intact across the cultural diversity of local rites. The answer is that there must be criteria or rules for judging the suitability and correctness of integrating local culture into the rite of Christian baptism. What are these criteria?

1. The foundational criterion is absolute fidelity to and preservation of the core of the baptismal shape. No form of inculturated baptism can dispense with washing in water and the invocation of the Blessed Trinity. This is the point of departure for the work of embellishing the rite through cultural dialogue and integration. It is also the point of arrival, in the sense that everything added to the rite is meant to draw attention to the core. We may say that cultural elements are integrated into the baptismal *ordo* not merely because they are meaningful and relevant to the local congregation, but above all because they are able to illustrate the core of baptism with catechetical clarity.

2. This leads us to a second criterion. We noted earlier that over a period of time the original shape or core of the baptismal rite developed through the assimilation of a great many cultural practices and traditions. We gathered from this that the church, in response to pastoral and cultural needs, took minute care to enrich the shape of baptism. Should this not be one of our basic liturgical criteria, namely that while we remain faithful to the original core, we should not thereby ignore the twenty centuries of ritual elaboration? It does not seem consonant with the church's post-apostolic tradition to reduce the baptismal rite to the bare essentials

of pouring three drops of water on the head of the candidate while the baptismal formulary is recited. Baptism is not only a celebration of faith: it also engages humans who are steeped in their culture and traditions.

The foregoing criterion requires that our work of inculturation take into account the full ritual shape of baptism. Concretely, this involves the following ritual items obtaining in the practice of a number of churches, though in varying degrees of importance: an introductory rite to welcome and name the candidate, proclamation of the word of God, prayer over the water (a tradition dating from the 3rd century), renunciation and profession of faith, baptismal bath with a trinitarian formulary, and some post-baptismal symbols like anointing (another 3rd-century rite), vesting and handing of lighted candles (rites introduced in the 4th century). Respect for these elements, even if they are not adopted, can draw churches together to their common origin, to traditions rooted in ages past. Communing with the past, especially in such a fundamental matter as baptism, reassures the local congregations, wherever and whenever they are established, that they come from long ago and provides them reason to claim a venerable origin.

3. The third criterion concerns the celebration itself, which includes the following: the presence of the Christian community; the role of the minister, parents (in the case of infant baptism) and sponsors; the appointed time for the celebration; and the use of the liturgical space and environment. It is not possible to deal here with these elements singly and at length. Suffice it to say that the community gathered for baptism represents the one holy, catholic and apostolic church into which the candidate is admitted. It is in the faith of this church, publicly professed by adult candidates or by parents and sponsors on behalf of the infant, that baptism is administered. Thus the inculturation of baptism should not foster tribal allegiance – though this is often at the heart of the indigenous rites of initiation – but communion with all Christian churches united in a common baptism and present here and now in the assembled community.

Furthermore initiation requires ministration. No one initiates himself or herself into a clan or tribe; no one becomes a Christian without the intervention of a minister. In normal practice the minister is one who is recognized by the church as the leader of the local congregation, or as one who functions on behalf of the church. In liturgical tradition the bishop took in hand the admission of catechumens, their progress or growth in the faith, their initiation through the rite of baptism and their post-baptismal instruction. In short, the entire process of becoming a Christian is a responsibility which the minister of baptism must bear. In sociological parlance, the role of the minister may be compared to the task of tribal leaders who "enculturate" a person into the ways of the tribe. This type of ministry is demanded by the nature of initiation, just as a child's birth and growth depend upon parenting. This is a criterion which any human society is able to appreciate.

Closely connected with the role of parents and sponsors is the naming of the person to be baptized. One might ask, what is in a name? The answer is, much. Christians are given a baptismal name by which God calls them as daughters and sons and the Christian community acknowledges their baptism. The name can be taken from the traditional list of Christian names or it can be an indigenous name which is traditional in one's culture. The use of an indigenous name can become a necessity in places where traditional Christian names are so inextricably associated with the politics of the West that they tend to isolate their bearers from the rest of society. On the other hand, there are people who object to indigenous names, especially when they evoke false worship, because they do not show the passage of the baptized from the old to the new dispensation.

Two other elements of the celebration are governed by criteria relating to time and space. Already in the 3rd century, as witnessed by Tertullian in his book *On Baptism*, the traditional days for solemn baptism were Easter and Pentecost, although in emergency situations any day, any hour, was considered suitable. In more recent times the other Sundays of the year began to share something of the eminence of Easter. There are authors who call ordinary Sunday "little Easter". Sunday in fact is regarded today as the "original feast day" of the Christian people. It is difficult to miss the strong symbolism Sunday confers upon the celebration of baptism, namely new creation (Sunday as the beginning of cosmogony) and new life (Sunday as the day of Christ's resurrection). It is useful to know that tribal initiations are normally timed to coincide with festivals and seasons of the year. By tradition the church assigns baptism to Sunday, especially Easter and Pentecost, because Sunday embodies every feast in the liturgical year.

Space and environment are other equally important elements of baptismal celebration. The 1st-century document called *Didaché* speaks of flowing water and hence of rivers and streams. By the 3rd century we read of pools or fonts, and somewhat later of baptistries. Initiation, especially in tribal tradition, is done in places set apart or marked for the purpose. Similarly, Christians are as a rule not re-born in water and the Spirit anywhere they chance to be, any more than they partake of the Lord's supper wherever they happen to set up a table. Suitable space and decorous environment are criteria, because in the liturgy God encounters us in "God's holy place".

4. The fourth criterion relates to the ritual formularies of baptism. A number of baptismal texts have come down to us from as early as the 3rd century, though allusions to some of them had been made in the 2nd century by Justin Martyr in his *First Apology*. The mystery rites which flourished before the 4th century initiated candidates with esoteric formularies. Tribal initiations also use them. Christian formularies were never meant to be esoteric, although in earlier times the formularies for baptism, as in the mystery rites, were kept secret even from the catechumens. This was by virtue of the *disciplina arcani* which reserved the "holy things" to the holy. But this discipline gradually fell into disuse as society in general was Christianized. The point is that baptismal formularies should be comprehensible when they are proclaimed in the assembly, and they should be able to announce clearly to the world the counter-cultural challenges of Christian baptism. Esoteric formularies found in some tribal initiatory rites do not serve as models for baptism.

There are several important baptismal texts which can be regarded as venerable because of their age. One is the formulary for the renunciation of the devil and his works and *pompae*. This latter word, which is somewhat difficult to translate, originally referred to the worship of idols which were carried in exuberant procession. There may be situations in which *pompae* can be rendered best by "false worship", which is defined as the cult of spiritual powers, the superstitious invocation of the spirits of the dead and the use of magical arts to obtain benefits. The formulary strongly signifies a radical break from sinful values and way of life. In one version of the 3rd-century apostolic tradition, the act of renunciation was done facing the west, the region of darkness, after which the candidate turned around (the symbol of *metanoia* or conversion) to face the east, the region of light.

Another formulary is the blessing of the baptismal water. Tertullian gives us the elements of the blessing: it is an invocation of God over the water in order that the Holy Spirit may make it holy. Once sanctified by the presence of the Holy Spirit, the water acquires the power to sanctify: it becomes a sacrament. Other formularies are the creed, which until the 9th century was used in the Western church in a triple question-and-answer form as the baptismal formulary; the actual baptismal formulary, which in its declarative form accentuates the ministerial role of the church; and the words that accompany the actions of anointing with chrism, vesting in white robe or other suitable colour and the handing of lighted candles. To this list of formularies we should evidently include those biblical texts that have baptismal content or message. In distant centuries the reading of the word of God was a prominent feature of the rites of catechumenate. In recent times the practice has become an integral part of the baptismal *ordo.*

The fourth criterion then, which refers to baptismal formularies, may be articulated as follows. The process of inculturation should take as point of departure the understanding the church has of the sacrament of baptism. The formularies, some of which date from very early times, are normally reliable bearers of what the church understands and communicates through the celebration. Before we consider creating new baptismal formularies for our local congregation, we should prudently examine what has traditionally existed and what is still kept in honour by churches in other parts of the world. In this way inculturation will foster unity with both the church's traditions and its present usages.

5. The fifth criterion governs the area of baptismal gestures and symbols. Tribal initiations are a veritable storehouse of powerful gestures and symbols. In the process of inculturation it can happen that these indigenous elements grab the lion's share in popular interest because of their dramatic, flamboyant and colourful appearance. Thus it is useful to recall that the primary gesture of baptism is the rather simple action of "washing in water". However, if it is fully performed through immersion, it can speak with power. Patristic writers like Ambrose of Milan equated immersion with burial: Christ was buried in the tomb, and so Christians are immersed in the water. Although the 1st-century *Didaché* envisaged affusion in places where water was scarce, subsequent liturgical books tended to give preference to immersion, even if just as a matter of lip service.

The primary symbol of baptism, on the other hand, is water. Again the *Didaché* tells us that if possible the water should be flowing. Flowing water is living water, and this symbol graphically illustrates the meaning of baptism as a life-giving sacrament. In those many cultures where water is not associated with initiation rites, its symbolic value might not be fully appreciated. Perhaps this is the reason why patristic writers and liturgical texts insistently recall the biblical passages concerning water (the water of creation, the deluge, the Sea of the Reeds, the water from the rock, the Jordan river and the water from the side of Christ). They do this in a bid to explain through biblical typology which water is used for the sacrament of rebirth. The criterion here is that only those indigenous symbols that are able to illustrate the meaning of baptismal water should be admitted into the *ordo*. Otherwise there is a real danger that they will push aside the essential baptismal symbol into the periphery of the rite.

6. A final criterion refers to the use of dynamic equivalence. This preferred method of inculturation is a type of translation in which the con-

tent or message of a rite, text or symbol transmitted from one people is re-expressed in the cultural form of another. Dynamic equivalence transmits the content by substituting a local equivalent for the original form. Through this method churches the world over remain united in a common understanding of the message of the baptismal *ordo*. However, the form bearing this shared message varies according to the culture of each locality. The method of dynamic equivalence can be used to great advantage when the content of the traditional *ordo* is judged to be timely, but the manner in which it is expressed is not consonant with the local culture. For example, vesting the newly baptized in a new garment speaks eloquently of acquired Christian dignity, of putting on Christ. But white does not speak in the same way to every culture. In some milieus white is the colour of mourning.

Conclusion

Obviously the foregoing baptismal elements and the criteria governing their inculturation do not all possess the same degree of importance. In their present form some baptismal elements may not even make sense to a given group. However, they all relate to the ideal shape of the baptismal *ordo* with the full complement of rites and symbols. They enhance in various ways the churches' understanding of the core of their common baptism. They render more explicitly what is merely implicit in the original "washing in water with the word". Lastly, they prove that diversity in unity is possible to achieve.

To sum up, inculturation diversifies the shape of baptism on account of cultural demand. This it does on the broad level of church communions. At the same time, however, it draws local congregations belonging to various communions closer together on account of their shared or common culture. These are the implications of inculturation for the unity of the church.

But inculturation also fosters unity across diversity. This it does by transmitting faithfully the core of baptism as well as the message of the traditional rites which have enriched that core over the centuries. In order that inculturation does not break the unity of churches in the core of baptism nor weaken their communion with received traditions, certain criteria need to be invoked. This was addressed in the second part of this paper.

BIBLIOGRAPHY

Roman Catholic liturgical documents

Congregation for Divine Worship, "Christian Initiation, General Introduction"; "Rite of Baptism for Children, General Introduction"; "Rite of Christian Initiation for Adults, General Introduction"; English texts in Thomas C. O'Brien, tr. and ed., *Documents on the Liturgy, 1963-1979 – Conciliar, Papal and Curial Texts*, International Commission on English in the Liturgy, Collegeville MN, Liturgical Press, 1982, pp.719-31,736-61.

Patristic literature

Ambrose of Milan, *De Sacramentis/De Mysteriis*, tr. and ed. by B. Botte, 4th ed., Paris, Cerf, 1994 (*Sources chrétiennes*, Vol. 25bis).

The Didaché, ed. by Willy Rordorf and André Tuilier, Paris, Cerf, 1978, c. 7 (*Sources chrétiennes*, Vol. 248).

Justin Martyr, *First Apology*, ed. L. Pautigny, Paris, A. Picard, 1904, c. 61; a partial English translation is found in W.A. Jurgens, ed., *The Faith of the Early Fathers: A Source-book of Theological and Historical Passages from the Christian Writings of the Pre-Nicene and Nicene Eras*, Collegeville MN, Liturgical Press, 1970.

La tradition apostolique de Saint Hippolyte: essai de reconstitution, ed., by B. Botte, 5th ed., Münster, Westfalen, Aschendorff, 1989, c. 21 (*Liturgiewissenschaftliche Quellen und Forschungen*, 39).

Studies

A. Chupungco, "Baptism in the Early Church and its Cultural Settings", in *Worship and Culture in Dialogue*, Geneva, Lutheran World Federation, Department for Theology and Studies, 1994, pp.39-56.

A. Chupungco, "The Future Shape of Sacramental Celebration", in *Liturgies of the Future*, New York, Paulist, 1989, pp.102-39.

Aidan Kavanagh, *The Shape of Baptism: The Rite of Christian Initiation*, New York, Pueblo Publishing, 1978.

Gordon Lathrop, "Baptism in the New Testament and its Cultural Settings", in *Worship and Culture in Dialogue*, pp.17-38.

Adrien Nocent, "L'initiation chrétienne", in *Le renouveau liturgique: Une relecture*, Paris, Beauchesne, 1993, pp.76-142.

On Baptism and the Spirit

The Ethical Significance of the Marks of the Church

VIGEN GUROIAN

As the church rounds the close of its second millennium, Christians must recapture the ecclesial and sacramental character of Christian ethics. They must see clearly once more that their ethics belongs to the mystery of the incarnation and the redemptive mission of the church. They must see afresh that their ethics issues directly from their adoption through baptism as sons and daughters of God. This is the work of the Holy Spirit, as the Spirit itself is present within the sacrament of baptism. And so, Christian ethics is also a gift of the Holy Spirit, and the kingdom of God is the proper horizon of the church's ethical striving. Some years ago I wrote that "baptism is where reflection upon Christian ethics ought to begin".[1] But this is not all that needs to be said about the relation of baptism and Christian ethics. By itself such a statement might leave the impression that baptism is simply a text which one mines when occasion demands in order to engage in the academic activity of writing Christian ethics; whereas baptism, rightly conceived, is a defining and self-constitutive practice of the church which is itself the wellspring of the church's ethics. Baptism gives "birth" to Christian ethics, much as it gives birth to new Christians, new ecclesial persons and the church itself, the body of Christ in the world.

This connection between baptism, ethics and the work of the Holy Spirit may seem obvious once it has been stated. But it is an insight that has been lost to much of contemporary Christian ethics. In many quarters this forgetfulness of the relation of ethics to sacrament has led to a confusion of Christian ethics with other human ethics grounded solely in reason. An impoverishment of pneumatology also lies at the source of this crisis in Christian ethics. This impoverishment is undoubtedly connected with the autonomies that both liturgical theology and Christian ethics have asserted in our time. The two disciplines have grown far apart from each other and rarely are engaged in serious conversation.

In 1982 an ecumenical landmark was achieved within world ecumenism when the Lima statement on *Baptism, Eucharist and Ministry* was issued. Through the commission on Faith and Order of the World Council of Churches a broad spectrum of churches agreed on common language regarding these essential characteristics of the church – baptism, eucharist and ministry. The BEM statement pushed strongly in the direction of re-grounding Christian ethics in liturgy, and in baptism particularly. It properly located the origin of Christian ethics in baptism. Likewise, it rightly identified the complete act of baptism-chrismation-eucharist as a work of the Holy Spirit. The key BEM passage reads as follows:

> In God's work of salvation, the paschal mystery of Christ's death and resurrection is inseparably linked with the Pentecostal gift of the Holy Spirit. Similarly, participation in Christ's death and resurrection is inseparably linked with the receiving of the Spirit. Baptism in its full meaning signifies and effects both... Christians differ in their understanding as to where the sign of the Spirit is to be found... All agree that Christian baptism is in water and the Holy Spirit (Baptism, para. 14).

Unfortunately, BEM's strong insight into the pneumatological character of baptism has caused hardly a ripple in the pond of Christian ethics. So it is with an eye towards remedying this absence of pneumatology in contemporary Christian ethics that I wish to discuss the baptismal origination and formation of Christian ethics.

A case in point

Stanley Hauerwas is perhaps the most influential Christian ethicist in the English-speaking world today. Not surprisingly, his work also suffers from a want of attention to pneumatology. When Hauerwas addresses the connection of sacraments and Christian ethics, his neglect of the Holy Spirit is conspicuous. For example, Hauerwas says this about the importance of baptism in the ethical life of Christians and the church:

> The sacraments enact the story of Jesus and, thus, form a community in his image. We could not be the church without them. For the story of Jesus is not simply one that is told: it must be enacted. The sacraments are means crucial to shaping and preparing us to tell and hear that story. Thus baptism is that rite of initiation necessary for us to become part of Jesus' death and resurrection. Through baptism we do not simply learn the story, but we become part of it.[2]

One should not underestimate the power of the biblical stories in the formation of the Christian life, and in his writings Hauerwas has done everyone a favour in reminding them of this. But it simply does not suffice to say that through the sacraments persons learn and become a part of a story. Who is to say that everyone in the church learns even the biblical story in the same manner? The story by itself does not have the power to make the church one and catholic. This unity and catholicity are the work of the Holy Spirit acting in and through those who call on the name of Jesus and together declare him Lord. The narrative is not a substitute for the Holy Spirit, and baptism in the Christian faith is the primal act through which human beings receive the gift of the Holy Spirit.

By baptism the sinful self is renewed and becomes a new ecclesial being with the seal of the Holy Spirit. Henceforth, this new Christian bears the church's marks of wholeness, holiness, catholicity and apostolicity. Baptism also incorporates the person into the mystical body of the church, which itself is an eschatological vehicle of the kingdom of God. The church owns a powerful story, rooted in scripture, which it perpetually recalls through liturgy and prayer. However, the church is first in the order of salvation. The story does not make the church or the Christian. The church and every living stone that comprises it makes, remembers, rehearses, proclaims and lives this story, which is without beginning or end, hidden in the mystery of the eternal God the Father, Son and Holy Spirit.

The church must call upon the Holy Spirit by name. Short of this, Christian ethics fails to embody and express the whole truth of the faith and to bring hope into a despairing world. The Orthodox baptismal prayers dynamically join pneumatology and remembrance as the church prepares to continue Christ's own redeeming work in the world. They invoke the Holy Spirit to come down at each and every baptism, as the Spirit did at Jesus' own baptism in the river Jordan and at Pentecost, so as to effect a radical change of heart and mind in every believer and help to bring about the kingdom of God.

Christian ethics and the Holy Spirit in the Armenian rite of holy baptism

The work of the modern ecumenical movement has affirmed all of this, and yet, as I have been saying, contemporary Christian ethics remains largely blind and deaf to its significance. In the vast corpus of Christian rites of baptism, few are as pneumatologically rich as the Armenian rite of holy baptism. This rite of my own church contains four hymns to the Holy Spirit, which appear at crucial moments within it. The second in the sequence, which is said over the font just before immersion, states the important truth that the Holy Spirit is the bringer of the "newness of life" (Rom. 6:4). The hymn contrasts baptism with the birth-giving of Eve, in this way also connecting the new birth through baptism with Mary's conception of the Son of God by the Holy Spirit. The hymn does not make the latter connection explicit – indeed, it does not mention Mary. However, the church remembers Eve as the "first mother" because the "second mother" is Mary, the Mother of God, the new Eve. Eve is the mother of the "old man" and Mary is the mother of the new humanity born of baptism and adopted in the Spirit as sons and daughters of God. The salient verses of the hymn read as follows:

> This day the sorrowful and nocturnal travail of the birth of the first mother has been loosed, for those who are born with body unto death and corruption have been born again by the Spirit to be sons of light of the heavenly Father; and therefore we bow down to the Father in spirit and truth.[3]

This is just one example of the pneumatological riches in the Armenian rite. It is significant also because, according to the rite, our ethical charge as Christians gains intelligibility only from the perspective of this new birth and adoption as sons and daughters of God and inheritors of God's kingdom. The prayer which is said over the holy oil (chrism) is even more explicit. It mentions the new people, the new spiritual body, to whom the newly baptized individual henceforth belongs: "Blessed art thou, O Lord God almighty, who has chosen for thyself a new people unto priesthood and kingship to be a holy nation and thy own people." Then it enumerates the virtues that the Holy Spirit plants within each new Christian. These gifts (or goods) of baptism assist the Christian through this life towards "the inheritance of the state of the saints in the light". The rite orders these goods carefully. The first that is named is "holiness of spiritual wisdom". This may be interpreted as the power that the Spirit gives to see the saving truth and apply it to life. Second is the "courage to struggle and triumph over the Adversary". Evil is in the world – and within each one of us – and has to be confronted as such before "turning" to the task of wholly conforming oneself to the pattern of Christ's own life. Faith needs courage to wage this spiritual struggle. The third good is the "strength to keep the commandments that enjoin virtuous deeds". This strength comprises such virtues as patience and perseverance. Finally, there is the "perfect discipline" to "honour" and glorify the Holy Trinity.[4] This prayer articulates an ethic for the church, an ecclesial ethic, and it makes our forgetfulness of baptism as the wellspring of Christian ethics seem that much more strange.

Baptism and the Spirit

But I have jumped ahead of myself. I must return to my central thread, which is the specific question about pneumatology and ethics, and reserve for later some comments about baptism and ethics and the new ecclesial person that is born within the baptismal waters. The text of Romans 6 is a centrepiece in all the Eastern rites of baptism and most Western rites as well. In this letter, the apostle declares that all Christians are baptized into Christ's death and resurrection, "so that we too might walk in the newness of life" (Rom. 6:4). The church distinguishes its baptism from the baptism of John the Forerunner in the important regard that John's baptism was purely of water for the repentance and remission of sins, whereas baptism in and with Christ *through water and Spirit* is a mystical and eschatological passage with Christ through death into the new life of the kingdom. Christologically speaking, this new kind of baptism is the church's principal expression of following Christ obediently in conformity to his perfected humanity.

Baptism and Christian ethics begin with the renunciation of Satan and a penitent turning from our fallen and discordant existence to a new way of holiness and peace patterned after Christ's relationship to the Father. But baptism and Christian ethics entail even more. A merely christological Christian ethics can err in several ways. For example, on the one hand, it can lapse into a totalistic belonging to the body under the strict regime of law or ecclesiastical authority; on the other hand, it might express itself, as in certain forms of liberal Protestantism, as an individualistic ethic of imitating the example of the ethical man named Jesus. But if we take the lead of scripture, we are able to avoid these mistakes and recapture the role of the Holy Spirit in Christian living. Once more the distinction between the baptism of Jesus and that of John is important. Only in the former is the Holy Spirit present, transforming the "old humanity" into the "new". The Acts of the Apostles relates that on Paul's first visit to Ephesus, he encountered several disciples whose understanding of baptism was indeed limited to the influence of John the Baptist. Luke continues:

> He [Paul] said to them, "Did you receive the Holy Spirit when you became believers?" They replied, "No, we have not even heard that there is a Holy Spirit." Then he said, "Into what then were you baptized?" They answered, "Into John's baptism." Paul said, "John baptized with the baptism of repentance, telling the people to believe in the one who was to come after him, that is, in Jesus." On hearing this, they were baptized in the name of the Lord Jesus Christ. When Paul had laid his hands on them, the Holy Spirit came upon them... (Acts 19:2-6).

So Christian baptism is baptism under the sign of the cross and of the Holy Spirit. A truly trinitarian Christian ethic acknowledges and reflects this pneumatological character of baptism. Centring Christian ethics eucharistically, as some have suggested, is not sufficient to recover this pneumatological dimension. The church constantly needs to recollect the coming of the Spirit in the washing with water and anointing with oil. Baptism and its perpetual recollection is essential, as is reflected in the communion prayer of the divine liturgy of the Armenian church. The prayer addresses the Father, "who hast called us by the name of thine Only-begotten and hast enlightened us through the baptism of the spiritual font" and asks him to "impress upon us the graces of the Holy Spirit, as thou didst upon the holy apostles, who tasted thereof and became cleansers of the whole world".[5] It is true that "Christ is sufficient", but only because he himself is obedient to the Father and does his will in all things and because he gives us the gift of his Holy Spirit. In the gospel of St John, Christ says: "He [the Father] will glorify me, because he will take what is mine and declare it to you. All that the Father has is mine. For this reason I said that he will take what is mine and declare it to you" (John 16:14-15).

In its strong pneumatological awareness, the Orthodox tradition understands chrismation as the completion of baptism. Baptism is itself epicletic; but chrismation is the completion of that action of the Spirit in baptism which launches each new Christian into the world for holy service. The Holy Spirit's work does not halt with baptism and wait for our next move. It continues to the logical conclusion, in which the Holy Spirit comes on the person as total gift, a personal Pentecost that is quite distinct from baptism and yet is also its completion, its fulfillment. Just as the Holy Spirit at Pentecost prepared the apostles to go out all over the world and pursue the calling of their own baptisms, so by being anointed with the oil every new Christian is readied to do the same. "It is the seal", writes Alexander Schmemann, "that preserves and defends in us the precious content and its fragrance; it is the sign of our high and unique calling."[6]

Baptism, ethics and the marks of the church

I have said that a new ecclesial person is born by baptism of water and the Spirit. This is a mystery that transcends empirical and biological categories of individuality. Baptism not only reveals anew what scripture already reports, that the human being is created in the image and the likeness of God. It also commences a process by which the image of God is in fact fully restored in each person, by virtue of God's own accomplishment of this for us through the incarnate Word. The 14th-century Byzantine theologian Nicholas Cabasilas comments on these mystical and ethical effects of the rite:

> When we come up from the water we bear the Saviour upon our souls, on our heads, on our eyes, in our very inward parts, on all our members – Him who

> is pure from sin, free from corruption, just as he was when he rose again and appeared to his disciples.[7]

The contemporary Orthodox theologian John Zizioulas has stated that the spiritual birth in the baptismal font constitutes the appearance of an ecclesial hypostasis (person), which is "a new mode of existence", replacing the biological hypostasis that is in bondage to the law of sin and subject to corruptible death. Baptism effects this change in the person immediately as well as proleptically, as this new mode of existence begins to grow and assimilate the old Adam into the new. 1 Peter 1:3-4 describes this: "By his [the Father's] great mercy, he has given us a new birth into a living hope through the resurrection of Jesus Christ from the dead, and into an inheritance that is imperishable, undefiled and unfading, kept in heaven for you." The completion of this process remains hidden in the mystery of God's own freedom and love. Nevertheless, it is an ascetical undertaking that we are called to here and now. Our complete rebirth and reconstitution into new ecclesial beings is contingent on constantly putting to death our old selfish selves for the love of God.

Baptism and the ecclesial character of Christian ethics

Let me return to a claim I made at the start – that through baptism the church itself is being born into the world. The church is born and renewed every time a new Christian is made; and by anointing with oil the Holy Spirit also confers all the essential marks of the church on that new Christian as gift and as calling. The church is one, holy, catholic and apostolic because through baptism the Spirit brings into existence whole, holy, catholic and apostolic persons. Again this is not an instantaneous or in any sense magical occurrence. The seed is sown with all its potential to grow into a healthy plant. The plant, however, must be nurtured and cultivated so that it will bear fruit. St Paul advised the Christians of Corinth that when a man joins himself to a prostitute he becomes united with her flesh. The archetype of personal union which this act perverts is the unity achieved by adherence to Christ performed and accomplished through baptism. The essence of the unity of the church is each new Christian's adherence to Christ. In like manner, the church is also holy. Yet it is holy only because the Spirit fills each new Christian at baptism and will not depart so long as the Spirit is welcomed. Indeed, what good is a body united and one if it is not also holy? The Armenian prayer of chrismation speaks of the person as "sanctified..., in the truth and in the light of the grace of the Holy Spirit, so that he [or she] may be a temple and a dwelling of thy Godhead and may be able to walk in all ways of righteousness".[8] Ethically speaking, the holiness of the church is a gift and also an ascetical undertaking of love, love that gives itself up even to death so that the other might live and be together with all in God and his kingdom.

The church is catholic. It is catholic because through baptism a new ecclesial way of being human is brought into existence which transcends every difference of race, culture, social status, and sex. Thus, St Paul writes:

> For in Christ Jesus you are all children of God through faith. As many of you as were baptized into Christ have clothed yourselves with Christ. There is no longer Jew or Greek, there is no longer slave or free, there is no longer male and female, for all of you are one in Christ (Gal. 3:26-28).

Catholicity, however, is neither mere universality nor multiculturality. In the first instance it is something not external but interior. It is Christ through the Holy Spirit abiding within the person. Catholicity concerns truth. It is the inward confirmation of the truth of salvation in Jesus Christ. This truth is given to every baptized Christian by the Spirit. All the virtues that are conferred by baptism and learned and practised through a life-long living and dying in Christ ought to serve this truth of salvation, and not the reverse. Whether this truth takes root and grows into catholic consciousness, however, depends on the nourishment and support of all who bear that truth within the community of the faithful.

In the Armenian prayer of chrismation, God, who is described as great and eternal and "know[ing] all secrets", and who is "holy and dwellest in the saints", is also named as the one who grants "the knowledge of thy truth to all them that believe in thee" giving "them the right to be sons of God through regeneration of water and spirit".[9] This describes the birth of the catholic mind of the church within each baptized person. It can be no other way. It is not the church as a human institution that gives the truth but God acting through the Spirit granting to each new Christian this truth through baptism. This truth is profoundly personal and yet it is also powerless unless shared and communicated by the entire community of faith.

And finally there is apostolicity. Apostolicity is both the handing on of tradition and the mission of the church into the world. The ethical force of this hardly needs to be described. At the close of the gospel of St Matthew Jesus gives his great commission to the apostles: "Go therefore and make disciples of all nations, baptize them in the name of the Father and the Son and of the Holy Spirit." This is the summation of all Christian ethics. For I do not think that there can possibly be Christian ethics unless there is mission and conversion. Yet even this apostolicity, this spirit of mission, first has to be born freely within the ecclesial baptized person. It is never an obligation imposed by the church upon the individual. The Holy Spirit must be active in each person, making that person free so that the church is apostolic as well, inspired to preach the gospel of salvation to all peoples. St John records that "Jesus said [to the disciples]..., 'Peace be with you. As the Father has sent me, so I send you'". But let us not forget what Christ then also did. When he had said this he breathed on them and said to them, 'Receive the Holy Spirit'" (John 20:21-23).

Conclusion

In conclusion, let me report that throughout this discussion of the ecclesial and ethical dimensions of baptism, I have tried to lend expression to a *broader* meaning of baptism than one single event in the life of a Christian, or even as a string of singular events that punctuate the normal rhythm of the church. Baptism should be seen as the concrete expression of a full life lived and dying daily in Christ. I mean this symbolically in the deepest sense of the Christian rite of baptism itself as death and burial and rebirth in Christ. But I also am speaking plainly. *Baptism encompasses the entire temporal life-span of a person.* It is beginning and end. We need to recapitulate and review, revisit and reflect upon our baptisms throughout our lives in order never to forget from whence we came and to whom our lives are finally bound and destined. In this manner, our ethics may become a complete way of life, a way of being in the world in service to the world and yet belonging entirely to God, and to God alone.

NOTES

[1] Vigen Guroian, *Incarnate Love*, Notre Dame IN, Univ. of Notre Dame Press, 1987, p.56.
[2] Stanley Hauerwas, *The Peaceable Kingdom*, Notre Dame IN, Univ. of Notre Dame Press, 1983, pp.107f.
[3] *The Order of Baptism: According to the Rite of the Armenian Apostolic Orthodox Church*, Evanston IL, St Nerses Seminary Press, 1964, p.31.
[4] *Ibid.*, p.33.
[5] *Divine Liturgy of the Armenian Apostolic Orthodox Church*, London, St Sarkis Church, 5th ed., rev., 1984, p.97.
[6] Alexander Schmemann, *Of Water and the Spirit*, Crestwood NY, St Vladimir's Seminary Press, 1974, p.80.
[7] Nicholas Cabasilas, *The Life in Christ*, Carmino J. De Catanzaro, Crestwood NY, St Vladimir's Seminary Press, 1974, p.62.
[8] *The Order of Baptism*, p.67.
[9] *Ibid.*, p.65.

Becoming a Christian: The Ecumenical Implications of Our Common Baptism

Report of the Consultation

I. Introduction

1. *"Blessed is the kingdom, of the Father, of the Son and of the Holy Spirit, now and ever, and unto ages of ages."*

These words begin the service of holy baptism in the Orthodox Church. As representatives of many churches the participants of this consultation affirm that baptism is rooted in the triune God into whose eschatological kingdom Christians are called. "He rescued us from the domain of darkness and brought us into the kingdom of his dear Son" (Col. 1:13).[1] Elsewhere St Paul writes, "for anyone united to Christ, there is a new creation: the old order has gone, a new order has already begun" (2 Cor. 5:17).

2. In our baptism we are joined to Christ and his body, the church. Our pathway is set and our journey to life eternal is begun, a journey which begins with our death and burial in the baptismal water. By the anointing and indwelling of the Holy Spirit, the life we live is no longer ours, but the life which Christ lives in us (Gal. 2:20).

3. In January 1997, during the time when Christians in many parts of the world celebrated the Week of Prayer for Christian Unity, an ecumenical group met at the Château de Faverges, Haute-Savoie, France. Gathered at the invitation of the Faith and Order Commission of the World Council of Churches, the fifteen participants came from the South and the North: from Papua New Guinea, Korea, India, Brazil, New Zealand, Finland, Germany, the United States, the United Kingdom, Jamaica, Ghana and Zaire. Many local churches were represented, of Anglican, Baptist, Disciples of Christ, Lutheran, Orthodox, Presbyterian, Roman Catholic and United Church traditions. The theme of the consultation was "Becoming a Christian: The Ecumenical Implications of Our Common Baptism". Among those present were liturgists, pastors and theologians sharing a common task: to consider the actual experience and practice of baptism in the life

of their churches, and how the churches might be encouraged to recognize each other's baptismal processes and liturgies as expressions of the one baptism which unites us with, and within, the one body of Christ.

4. The consultation focused on three main issues:

- the *ordo* (the fundamental structure or pattern) of baptism in its broadest sense, including instruction (catechesis), the act of water washing, and the continuing, life-long process of growth into Christ;
- the inculturation of baptism, through which its meaning, and the irreducible elements of the baptismal rite, are expressed through the means particular to each culture; and
- the "ethical economy" of baptism, or the implications of the process of baptism for the ethical formation, reflection and action of Christians.

5. The first two of these issues, those of *ordo* and inculturation, have been treated in relation to worship generally in an earlier ecumenical consultation entitled "So We Believe, So We Pray: Towards Koinonia in Worship".[2] Held by Faith and Order in Ditchingham, England, in 1994, this consultation reflected the increasing awareness of the central importance of worship for the ecumenical movement in general, and for the search for Christian unity in particular. It explored the theological implications of the "liturgical renewal" of recent decades, as well as the implications, for worship of the growing body of theological agreements among the churches. For Faith and Order it meant the renewed awareness of *liturgical practice* as a crucial dimension of the faith, life and witness of the church.[3]

6. At Faverges the issues of the *ordo* and inculturation were explored in relation to *baptism* in its broadest sense, and to present-day baptismal practice in the churches. These topics are closely inter-related: the baptismal *ordo* provides the basis and touchstone for the inculturation of baptism, while the process of inculturation should express the meaning and pattern of baptism in a way that illuminates, rather than obscures, its reality. The third issue treated at Faverges, the inter-relation of baptism and ethics, was a new element in the discussion (the relation of ethics to worship generally had been noted, but not pursued, at Ditchingham).[4] Ethics belongs inescapably, however, to reflection on baptism understood as initiation into the community of believers, and as a life-long process of growth in Christian identity and discernment. Indeed the meaning of Christian baptism and the nature of the ritual actions associated with it are normative for Christian ethics, even as the process of inculturation has an ethical dimension and significant ethical implications.

II. The *ordo* of baptism

7. Our churches live with different histories. Some are national churches whose people naturally bring their children for baptism. Other churches have separated themselves from state and nation, and in them baptism is distinct from local (parish) or national custom. Other churches find themselves in situations of new missionary opportunity, the great majority of their candidates for baptism being first-generation Christians. Other churches, in older missionary contexts, are challenged by new emphases on the Spirit and baptism. Yet other churches find themselves in a shifting scene as their societies become increasingly "post-Christian".

8. Thus we find baptismal practice is often shaped by pastoral and missiological considerations as well as by doctrine. Indeed, our theology is often developed in order to describe the pastoral need. So history and context inspire theological insight as under the Spirit the church seeks to apply the ministry of Christ to the particularities of the human situation. Theology and practice do not exist in a vacuum.

A. Recognition of one another's baptism

9. There are two ways in which we may learn to recognize one another's baptism. One is to convert everybody else to our theology and practice. The other is to understand how our baptismal practices are responses to different pastoral and missionary contexts as well as responses to God's call in Christ.

10. An important ecumenical question is, "What are the criteria for mutual recognition of baptism?" In the past many have proposed theological criteria for such recognition. But baptism is more than doctrine alone. In this consultation we have sought to identify criteria which arise from baptism as rite and pattern of life. This way of thinking we call *ordo*, by which we mean baptism as call to life in Christ and map for pilgrimage to Christ's new creation.

11. The Faith and Order convergence text *Baptism, Eucharist and Ministry* (BEM), published by the World Council of Churches in 1982,[5] has become one of the most widely read and discussed ecumenical texts in modern times. This text, itself the fruit of many years of ecumenical study and discussion, has helped to create a new ecumenical situation. Through the BEM process of study and response many churches have gained renewed understanding and enrichment of their own faith, have engaged in ecumenical learning and have developed new relationships with other churches.

12. As a convergence statement, BEM calls for common affirmations by divided churches struggling towards visible unity. According to Faith

and Order's report on the official responses of the churches to BEM, there is "a firm agreement that baptism, eucharist and ministry are all rightly understood as enacted and enabled by God in the unity of Father, Son and Holy Spirit".[6]

13. BEM emphasizes the significance of baptism for koinonia (communion), stating that:

> Through baptism, Christians are brought into union with Christ, with each other and with the church at every time and place. Our common baptism, which unites us to Christ in faith, is thus a basic bond of unity. We are one people and are called to confess and serve one Lord in each place and in all the world (Baptism, para. 6).

14. In their responses to BEM churches generally affirmed an impressive degree of agreement and convergence on baptism. Virtually all agree that by God's grace and power the baptized person is incorporated into Christ's body and anointed by the Holy Spirit. Many also agreed that "our one baptism into Christ constitutes a call to the churches to overcome their divisions and visibly manifest their fellowship" (Baptism, para. 6). In many places, although questions of eucharist and ministry persist, churches have entered into formal agreements regarding mutual recognition of baptismal practice.

15. Divisions, however, still remain; and some churches have difficulty in mutually recognizing their various practices of baptism as sharing in the one baptism in Christ. For example, those who describe themselves as "believer baptists" often appear to deny that infants baptized in other churches are believers, while many who practise such baptism declare that it, too, is "believer's baptism". For them, children – even infants – are believers: God enables them to believe, or the church believes with them and for them. For some, despite the help provided in BEM, infant baptism remains a significant obstacle to mutual recognition; for others, there is significant disagreement as to where in the baptismal process the gift of the Holy Spirit is to be found – in the water rite, in chrismation or in the laying on of hands, or in the combination of all three actions. There are other areas of disagreement which may hinder growth towards koinonia on the basis of mutual recognition of baptism.

16. The present text attempts to provide a basis which may help churches to move beyond what has already been achieved. Two starting points are found in BEM. The first is the recognition that "baptism is related not only to momentary experience but to life-long growth into Christ... The life of the Christian is necessarily one of continuing struggle yet also of continuing experience of grace" (Baptism, para. 9). The second is the awareness that baptism takes place within the community

of faith, requires personal confession of faith, and points to and is founded on the faithfulness of God (Baptism, para. 12).

B. The common baptismal ordo

17. The Ditchingham report (see para. 5 above) suggests that the *ordo* (pattern) of Christian worship may be immensely helpful in the ongoing discussion of many of the issues which still divide Christian churches. By *ordo* is meant "the undergirding structure which is to be perceived in the ordering and scheduling of the most primary elements of Christian worship", an ordering "which roots in word and sacrament held together".[7] Among these basic structures of Christian worship are patterns of word and table, of catechetical formation and baptism. Recognition of these patterns – founded in the New Testament, attested to in the ancient sources of both the Christian East and the Christian West, practised today in diverse forms in different churches – gives us a basis for a mutually encouraging conversation between the churches.

18. This conversation may challenge the churches to re-examine the ways in which they express these basic structures of Christian worship. In the words of the Ditchingham report:

> Churches may rightly ask each other about the local inculturation of this *ordo*. They may call each other towards a maturation in the use of this pattern or a renewed clarification of its central characteristics or, even, towards a conversion to its use.[8]

What is clear is that the patterns of Christian worship, including the pattern (*ordo*) of baptism, provide a major basis for koinonia between local churches and for a koinonia spanning both time and space.

19. According to the Ditchingham consultation, this *ordo* of Christian worship includes the great outline of baptism, understood as "formation in faith and baptizing in water together, leading to participation in the life of the community".[9] These linked actions of baptism are seen by that report as part of the ancient yet ever-new patterns which the churches already possess, which they are invited to recognize in each other and renew in themselves.

20. But this great pattern of baptizing (formation in faith, baptism in water and life in community) is not simply the discovery of modern ecumenical conversation. It is found already in the witness of the scriptures. At Pentecost, according to Acts 2, baptisms *follow* from Peter's preaching and *lead* those baptized to life in the community: "They devoted themselves to the apostles' teaching and fellowship, to the breaking of bread and the prayers" (2:42) as well as to the distribution of goods to those in need (2:45). Those who heard, who were baptized and entered

the community's life, were already made witnesses of and partakers in the promises of God for the last days: the forgiveness of sins and the outpouring of the Holy Spirit on all flesh (2:38). Similarly, in what may well be a baptismal pattern, 1 Peter testifies that proclamation of the resurrection of Jesus Christ and teaching about new life (1:3-21) lead to purification and new birth (1:22-23). This, in turn, is followed by eating and drinking God's food (2:2-3), by participation in the life of the community – the royal priesthood, the new temple, the people of God (2:4-10) – and by further moral formation (2:11ff.). At the beginning of 1 Peter the writer sets this baptism in the context of obedience to Christ and sanctification by the Spirit (1:2). So baptism into Christ is seen as baptism into the Spirit (cf. 1 Cor. 12:13). In the fourth gospel, Jesus' discourse with Nicodemus indicates that birth by water and Spirit becomes the gracious means of entry into the place where God rules (John 3:5).

21. Such a reading of the New Testament helps us to interpret the baptismal practices of local churches in the first several centuries of Christian history. The patterns of the New Testament became the *ordo* of the churches. Preaching and teaching leading to baptism have shaped the *catechumenate*: candidates, teachers and sponsors engaged in the formation in faith. The great washing with water and the Spirit, leading those so washed into participation in the eucharist and in the life of the community, became the central event of *baptism*, often held on Easter Eve or at Epiphany or at other great feasts, often accompanied with signs of the Spirit who is active in baptism. And the continued *life in community* came to be experienced at every Sunday eucharist, as the assembly of the baptized, and in the exercise of witness and mission, and in the care for the poor. While the expression of this pattern already knew diversity in the early centuries – for example, in the length of the process and in the secondary ritual signs added to it – the Christian pattern itself was remarkably similar and recognizable across the churches. Those baptized in Antioch recognized those baptized in Carthage and Rome as members of the one body of Christ. This pattern was not simply an educational programme of the churches but a witness to, and participation in, the eschatological promise of God. It was constantly accompanied by prayer, by fasting as waiting on God, by blessings and exorcisms spoken over the candidates, by a great thanksgiving over the water itself. It expressed and fostered a continued sense that the triune God was acting here.

22. Furthermore, the long process of formation in faith (the catechumenate), baptism and incorporation into community was itself summed up in the central events of the baptismal rite. The renunciations of evil and the confession of faith – the creed – summarized and stood for the

whole catechumenate. The reception of candidates into the community, the kiss of peace and the first eucharist, could anticipate the whole Christian life. What is more, the *ordo* of catechumenate, baptism and incorporation is constantly echoed in the whole Christian existence. In the life-long learning of the faith of Christ the catechumenate continues. In daily dying and rising Christians reclaim their baptism into the death and resurrection of Christ. In repeated reconciliation in the church the baptized are restored to community. In the celebration of worship the church is renewed for the mission of Christ and formed in the patterns of Christian ethics. This reflection of Christian life, of life in Christ, in the baptismal process and this summary and anticipation of the process in the central baptismal events demonstrate a phenomenon known in ritual studies as "recapitulation". Baptism recapitulates the *ordo*. The *ordo* recapitulates the Christian life. Christians find the deepest reality of this baptismal recapitulation in the faith that the Triune God, who creates and saves all things, is present and active here. By means of God's continuing grace and presence baptism is *process* and once-for-all eschatological *event* and *pattern* for all of life.

23. Christian history has sometimes seen an apparent dismemberment of the matters which Acts 2 and 1 Peter hold together. Baptism has often been separated from catechesis and from eucharist and community life. The actual water-bath and admission to the Lord's table have frequently been dissociated. Confirmation has sometimes been held years after baptism itself, without baptismal reference. The process of baptism has too seldom known relationship to life in its many dimensions, not least the ethical. In many instances water-baptism and the gift of the Spirit have been disconnected, often becoming two "baptisms". The baptismal processes of the various churches have too often been dislocated from one another to the point that the churches have been unable to recognize in one another's practice the one baptism into Christ.

24. We are assisted towards common renewal and mutual recognition by a recovery of the *ordo*, a recovery of the vision of Acts 2 and 1 Peter as underlying the practice of the churches. Churches of different traditions can use this great *ordo* (shape or pattern) of the baptismal reality to interpret and refresh their own practices, and to recognize the diverse gifts of baptismal understanding and practice which may be present in other churches. Thus, some churches have strongly maintained a practice of teaching and the making of disciples. Others have exercised the sacramental signs at the heart of baptismal celebration with a vivid strength. Others have found fresh signs of new life in Christ in their own local contexts, signs which have enriched the general Christian understanding of baptism. Others have shown us the way to practise ongoing reconcili-

ation to community life. Clearly the churches have much to learn from one another's distinctive gifts and witness.

C. Towards renewal and mutual recognition of baptism

25. In matters of *renewal*, the *ordo* may assist the churches to ask themselves the following questions, as many are already doing.

a) Concerning the catechumenate:

- Are we holding baptism and formation in faith sufficiently together?
- Can we welcome again the ministry of catechists and restore the importance of baptismal sponsors among us?
- Can sponsors actively accompany every adult coming to baptism and uniting with the church's life?
- Can sponsors also accompany those who cannot answer for themselves as well as the parents or others who may be bringing these little ones?
- Can such catechists and sponsors be trained and assisted by the prayers of the whole congregation?
- Can we recover the catechumenate, or a pattern like the catechumenate, for both adult candidates and for those who are bringing children?
- Can we pray regularly in the Sunday assembly for all the candidates for baptism, strongly claiming them already as Christ's own and strongly asking the Spirit to cast all evil out of their lives?
- In churches which do not baptize infants, can the children be enrolled and blessed and accompanied towards their own day of baptism?

b) Concerning the baptismal rite itself:

- Can we practise a strong use of water for all candidates, recovering immersion fonts where possible?
- Can we always hold our baptisms in the presence of the church – or of representatives of the church – letting the whole assembly gather around the place of the water?
- Can we reclaim the great Christian festivals, especially Easter and Epiphany, as particularly appropriate times for baptism?
- Can we understand the principal minister of baptism as ordinarily the presider in a local assembly of Christians – someone authorized and recognized by the wider church – acting in and with that assembly?
- Can we declare in our rites that the Spirit of God is poured out on these new members of the body of Christ, whether by the laying on of hands, sealing with the sign of the cross (signation) or anointing with oil (chrismation)?

- Can we lead all the newly baptized immediately to participation in the eucharist?
- Can we consider together whether any secondary signs – other anointings or new clothing or other local expressions of new life in Christ – can further unfold the meaning of the *ordo* itself?

c) Concerning incorporation into the life of the community:
- Can we assist the baptized to find their place in the mission and service of the church, the expression of their baptismal vocation?
- Can we enable a life-long learning of the faith, by all people – clergy and laity, old and young, old-timers and newcomers – together, side by side in our churches?
- Can sponsors and catechists continue to accompany children baptized in infancy in a post-baptismal catechesis which helps them to appropriate their own baptismal gift of faith?
- Can we find occasions to remember our baptism, celebrate its powerful gift and renew our own promises, occasions which may occur in persons' lives at moments of crisis, change or renewal?
- Can we see every Sunday eucharist as the repeated remembrance and renewal of baptism?

And can we do these things by teaching, love and invitation, opening up and strengthening what is already in our churches, and not by constraint and compulsion?

26. In matters of *recognition*, the *ordo* may assist the churches to ask themselves the following questions:
- Can we see this great pattern operative in our own and in other churches? Can we treasure ways each church may have been able to give special emphasis to certain parts of the *ordo* – even while calling each other to a recovery of fullness in our understanding and practice?
- Can churches which baptize infants trust in the blessing and dedication of children among those who baptize only believers who can answer for themselves, seeing these children as in a rich catechumenate of long duration?
- Can churches which baptize believers who can answer for themselves trust the recovery of catechumenate and life-long learning among the churches which baptize infants, as a sign of their baptismal seriousness?
- Can all churches, whatever their formula of baptism, acknowledge that the whole *ordo* and all of its catechesis must express the triune Name?
- Can we ensure that our catechesis teaches, and our rites express, that baptism is always into Christ's whole body?

And can such reflections and new patterns of thinking about baptism as *ordo* foster new, creative and trustful ways to approach old controversies over recognition and re-baptism?

27. Our answers to these enquiries may lead the churches to ask themselves questions which could change their way of living with one another:

- Are there matters of renewed baptismal practice which divided local churches could begin undertaking together?
- Could a renewed catechumenate (the process of forming in faith) or a training of catechists and sponsors be undertaken together?
- Could we be present at each other's baptisms, whether through representatives or as entire congregations?
- Could we do baptism together, side-by-side, at great feasts we have in common?
- Could local churches provide a common baptismal certificate?
- Could we consider constructing a common font or baptistry for the local churches in a town or village?

And could we begin to do some of these things out of love, out of new insights into the *ordo*, out of the conviction that through baptism the Holy Spirit ever draws us into koinonia, into the very unity and life of the Triune God?

III. The inculturation of baptism

28. The Christian faith is rooted in God's act of incarnation: "The Word became flesh and dwelt among us" (John 1:14). Consistent with this is the fact that the universal truth of the gospel is everywhere experienced and expressed in local language and cultural forms. This happens through the process of inculturation. The Ditchingham report defined inculturation in part as "a form of creative activity accountable to both received liturgical tradition and the actual praxis of the church as well as to the integrity of culture...".[10] Inculturation, therefore, is the use of cultural means in order to express the meaning of worship in a way that helps people within a specific context to come to a clearer understanding and experience of the mystery of God's love. It is a way of growing in understanding.

29. Thus inculturation is a complex process. It comes out of the community in which it is happening and cannot be imposed from outside.

30. Because inculturation has also the potential of obscuring the Christian message, careful discernment is necessary.[11] For this the following principles and criteria may be helpful.

A. The inculturation of worship in general

31. The Ditchingham report developed a number of principles for the inculturation of worship.[12] These principles have the following practical implications:

- The starting point for inculturation is the basic *ordo* or "shape" of worship as a gift of God.
- Appropriate inculturation cannot occur without an understanding of the meaning of Christian worship, as the purpose of inculturation is to lead to a deeper understanding of that meaning.
- Inculturation also requires a deep knowledge of and familiarity with the specific culture in which it occurs, paying attention to the ethos, cultural values and needs of particular communities.
- Inculturation must take account of the fact that "culture" itself is a difficult concept. Cultures are complex and developing, dynamic rather than static. Many cultures today face extreme pressures, both external and internal, from economic forces and challenges to traditional values and practices. In some settings there is conflict between dominant and subordinate cultures, and within a specific culture some voices may have been silenced.
- The inculturation of worship should not encourage ethnocentrism or cultural imperialism, both of which are contrary to the Christian gospel.
- Basic to inculturation is the understanding that the whole creation is given to us as a means of coming into communion with God. Therefore in Christian worship material elements such as water, bread and wine are used to bring people into this communion. In the process of inculturation, language, symbols and signs of a specific culture are used in Christian worship in a way that goes beyond their original meaning. They are transformed as they are used for professing Jesus Christ.
- But inculturation includes also a counter-cultural aspect. Baptism calls Christians into a new life: the baptized live in the world but do not belong to it (John 15:19). This means the transformation of their former life and religious and ethical orientation (see para. 43 below and BEM, Baptism, para. 4). It may even mean a break with the family, in cases where there is a conflict between the values of the family and those of the gospel. Therefore the line between church and society, and the relationship between them, has to be clear. We must carefully distinguish which cultural elements are helpful and which are not. The main criterion for this has to be whether these elements serve Jesus' double commandment to love God and neighbour (Matt. 22:34-40).

- Inculturation therefore is dynamic and has to happen in continuous dialogue between the gospel and local culture.
- The process of inculturation requires a certain humility which is open to learn from others and their insights. Churches can learn from one another's experience in this process. This therefore requires an ecumenical awareness of belonging together with other churches to the one body of Christ. The process of inculturation needs to occur in dialogue with other churches in a spirit of mutual accountability.

B. Baptism in the Christian tradition

32. Christian baptism arose from the baptism of John the Baptist and has therefore a reference to other washing rites existing at that time. But Christian baptism had, from the beginning, some specific characteristics which distinguished it from purification or initiation rites. In this sense Christian baptism is itself the result of inculturation. We see this process continued in the development of baptismal space, including baths or fonts of different kinds as appropriate to the particular cultural setting.

33. As seen in paragraphs 17-22 above, emerging from the tradition is a basic *ordo* or pattern of baptism: formation in faith and baptizing in water leading to participation in the life of the community. This *ordo* has been developed liturgically in different ways in the different Christian traditions.

34. Of special interest is the celebration of the water rite. The Ditchingham report points out that the basic liturgical components of this rite which emerge from tradition are "proclamation of the scripture; invocation of the Holy Spirit; renunciation of evil; profession of faith in the Holy Trinity; and the use of water in the name of the Father and of the Son and of the Holy Spirit".[13] Over time, as the rite became incultured, these elements were expressed in different ways. In some cases additional rites and symbols were added, such as an introductory rite to welcome and name the candidate, prayers over the water and some post-baptismal symbols like anointing, vesting and the handing over of lighted candles.

35. Cultural elements such as music, musical instruments, architecture, language using specific images and allusions according to the context, and other symbols have also been added. This process continues to the present day.

C. Criteria for the inculturation of baptism

36. As emphasized in paragraphs 16 and 22 above, baptism is not a punctiliar event but a process of growth. The inculturation of baptism includes all stages of this process.

37. Criteria are needed to discern which cultural elements may help to illuminate the fundamental meaning of baptism and which would otherwise obscure it. The responses to BEM reported "contextual challenges in baptism" coming especially from churches in Africa and Asia. However, all churches live in specific cultural contexts and therefore all are challenged to exercise discernment.

38. The following criteria for the inculturation of baptism follow the principles for inculturation of worship in general. They result from reflection on the actual process of inculturation occurring in different churches today.

39. *Criteria for the inculturation of the ordo of baptism:*

- The inculturation of baptism needs fidelity to and preservation of the fundamental *ordo* of baptism as it was developed in the tradition and described above. No form of incultured baptism can dispense with the basic elements of the baptismal *ordo*: formation in faith, washing in water and participation in the life of the community.
- The inculturation of baptism will look for gestures, signs and symbols in a specific culture which relate to the essential aspects of baptism, such as its meaning as incorporation into the body of Christ and as conferring a life-long new status.

An example is a church in Burkina Faso whose entrance is built in the form of a traditional mask used for initiation. The congregation enters the church through the mouth of this mask. The original meaning of the mask, symbolizing the other world, is transformed through a cross that is above it on the top of the church. The mask in its new, Christian context signifies: this is the place of being newly born.

To give another example, in Zaire the candidate for baptism is passed or passes through the legs of the godfather or godmother. This sign of putting oneself in the protection of someone else is a particular cultural expression of sponsorship for baptism.

40. In some regions the use of traditional initiation symbols in baptism by some denominations creates new separations between churches. In order to avoid this, the inculturation of baptism should happen in mutual respect and mutual accountability to other churches, in such a way that local churches are united in cultural expressions rather than separated.

41. *Criteria for the inculturation of the water rite:*

- The basic water rite may be embellished in different ways through inculturation, but anything added to the rite should draw attention to its fundamental meaning, illuminating and explicating this rather than obscuring it.

- The ritual elaboration of the baptismal rite during the centuries of the early church should be respected, even if these elements are not adopted. Through such respect churches may acknowledge their common origin.
- The inculturation of baptism will take into account the role of time and space for the celebration. Christians should be encouraged to baptize on a Sunday or a traditional Christian feast day even if there are cultural pressures against this.
- The space and environment for baptism have to be culturally appropriate. For some situations this may mean the use of lakes or rivers, for others the use of baptismal baths or fonts.

  In some places in the early church, for example, baptismal fonts (pools in the ground) were built in the shape of a cross or a tomb in order to point to the meaning of baptism as incorporation into Christ's death.

- Festal vestments can express and enrich the festal character of baptism.

  In some cultures, for example, baptismal vestments are white, but in others red is a more appropriate colour for celebration.

- The inculturation of baptism will take into account the role of the minister, the parents and the congregation and will express the community-building potential of baptism.
- The community gathered for baptism represents the one holy, catholic and apostolic church into which the candidate is admitted. Thus the inculturation of baptism should transcend any group allegiance and lead into communion with God and with all Christian churches united in a common baptism. Prayers and hymns may be used to express this.
- The inculturation of baptism involves the search for language in the formularies which is understood by the people in that specific context.

  For example in Korea, where filial piety plays an enormous role, the questions the candidate is asked in the baptismal rite should be formulated in a way that reflects this piety. A possibility would be a formulation like: "Will you commit yourself to Jesus Christ as the head of your new life?"

- The inculturation of baptism will look for gestures, signs and symbols in a specific culture which relate to the essential aspects of baptism.

A powerful example comes from Zaire, where the meaning of death and resurrection in the water rite of baptism is illuminated through an additional rite where the candidate is covered with banana leaves, while a penitential or mourning song is struck up. Then the priest takes the candidate's right arm, raising him and shouting: "Christ has risen from the tomb, living forever. You too, live with him; arise."

Another example from Zaire is the anointing with white kaolin *(a chalky substance) which is put on the arms, the cheeks, the feet, illustrating blessing, the attainment of a new status in life and the belonging to the new, victorious world.*

42. Inculturation involves a risk, the risk of "the Word made flesh". As Christians we must take this risk, inspired by the Lord, the Holy Spirit, as we use all our human resources to express our faith.

IV. Baptism and ethics

43. The Baptism section of *Baptism, Eucharist and Ministry* stresses the ethical dimension of baptism, as well as the fundamental inter-relation of baptism and ethics. Thus BEM notes:

> The New Testament underlines the ethical implications of baptism by representing it as an ablution which washes the body with pure water, a cleansing of the heart of all sin, and an act of justification (Heb. 10:22, 1 Pet. 3:21, Acts 22:16, 1 Cor. 6:11). Thus those baptized are pardoned, cleansed and sanctified by Christ, and are given as part of their baptismal experience a new ethical orientation under the guidance of the Holy Spirit (Baptism, para. 4; cf. para. 32 above).

And again:

> As they grow in the Christian life of faith, baptized believers demonstrate that humanity can be regenerated and liberated. They have a common responsibility, here and now, to bear witness together to the gospel of Christ, the Liberator of all human beings. The context of this common witness is the church and the world... they acknowledge that baptism, as a baptism into Christ's death, has ethical implications which not only call for personal sanctification, but also motivate Christians to strive for the realization of the will of God in all realms of life (Rom. 6:9ff.; Gal. 3:27-28; 1 Pet. 2:21-4:6) (Baptism, para. 10).

These passages state forcefully the ethical implications of Christian baptism, showing how both growth in personal sanctification and ethical engagement within the world are necessary expressions of the faith into which we are baptized.

44. But it is not only that baptism has certain ethical implications for both personal and social life. More fundamentally, the meaning of Chris-

tian baptism and the nature of the ritual acts associated with it are *normative for Christian ethics itself*, and this in two ways. First, baptism as a life-long process of incorporation into Christ leads inevitably to an ethic rooted in and oriented towards life within community. Second, baptism as focused in the ritual action of dying and rising again leads inevitably to an ethic rooted in and oriented to a life of self-giving service. What does it mean that baptism is a process of initiation into a *community of faith*? And what does it mean that the metaphor for the central ritual act of baptism is that of *dying and rising to new life*? These questions point the way to understanding the basic nature and quality of Christian ethics.

45. This perspective helps clarify the intrinsic relation of ethics to both the *ordo* and inculturation of baptism. The classic process or *ordo* of baptism, the recovery of which has been discussed in paragraphs 17-22 above, can be seen as a process of ethical formation. The candidates for baptism are invited to turn from the values of a world seen apart from God; they are concretely taught new values of justice and love. The very act of baptism involves an immersion in Christ and thus a dying to the old life. And the water-rite leads to community and to care for the poor, to participation in the life and mission of the community as it bears witness to the truth about God and the truth about the world which is beloved by God. The continued remembrance of baptism and the "life-long catechumenate" offer occasions for the refreshment of these values.

46. There is also an ethical dimension to the process of the inculturation of baptism. Every act of inculturation involves a choice – whether conscious or unconscious – about which cultural elements and values are best suited to embody and illuminate the meaning of baptism and its focal ritual acts. Such choices are not neutral, as we recognize increasingly from the history of Christian mission. Instead of enabling the Christian gospel to take root in local soil, inculturation may serve as the vehicle for the values of a dominant, foreign culture to suppress local culture, or it may help one element within local culture to become dominant over others. Thus a Christian ethical analysis of each process of inculturation is also needed, to ensure that inculturation reflects the values of the gospel. This applies, of course, to far more than baptism, but baptism is of special importance because it is the way in which persons enter the church, and because of its relation to traditional rites of passage.

A. Baptism as ethical formation

47. Baptism is the wellspring of Christian ethics. Christian ethics comes into existence because Christians are born again of water and

Spirit in the life of Christ Jesus crucified and resurrected. Nevertheless, Christian moral reflection and ethics have increasingly grown apart from the *lex orandi* (the rule of prayer) and asserted their own autonomy. With an awareness of the dangers inherent in this trend, interest has arisen in some quarters to consider the eucharist or Lord's supper as the locus of moral formation and discernment, but very little has been said about *baptism* and ethics. This lack of ethical reflection on the meaning of baptism and on the baptismal practices of the churches is puzzling in view of the fact that scripture and the earliest Christian sources, whether Cyril of Jerusalem, Ambrose of Milan or John Chrysostom, strongly suggest the potential in baptism and associated catechetical instruction for moral formation in the churches.

48. Baptism is "moral pedagogy", ethical instruction for the people of God. Its ethic is an ethic of humility and love one for the other, a participation by grace in the divine life (2 Pet. 1:4). The selfish self dies in the baptismal waters and a new self motivated by love (agape) is born, reconciled to God and to others, even the enemy, always dying in Christ in order to give birth to life.

49. We are claimed by Christ in baptism, signed and sealed by it, for the entirety of our lives. The sacrament of baptism is administered to a person once. But the grace it bestows and the transformation it begins encompass the whole of the Christian's life, and this not in isolation but joined to Christ and in the communion of his body. Our baptism takes us back to Christ's own baptism, and forward into the kingdom he announced and which is present in Christ's body, the church. At every baptism the Holy Spirit pours grace upon us, as at the River Jordan when the Spirit rested upon Jesus in the form of a dove and when, with wind and fiery tongues, the apostles and others gathered at Pentecost. This is shown forth in the Armenian rite of baptism, in which the holy chrism is poured into the water of the font from a vessel that is in the shape of a dove, thus recalling Jordan and Pentecost, so that every baptism is also the "baptism of the church". Thus the church is renewed and reawakened to its mission. A hymn of the Holy Spirit completes this vision:

Blessing in the highest
to him that proceedeth from the Father,
to the Holy Spirit,
through whom the apostles
drank the immortal cup
and invited the earth to heaven.[14]

50. Baptism leads to the communion cup precisely because baptism is an entry into the eternal communion of saints and the beginning of the

church's mission to enlighten all of humankind with the light that is life. Those who practise conversion baptism remind the church that each time they gather around the table they remember how they got there. For them, as for others, the Lord's supper recapitulates the moment of their conversion and decision to live the life in Christ. Baptism and the Lord's supper so understood encompass the whole life of a Christian. That life, from new birth and beginning in baptism through physical death, is understood from the perspective of dying and being reborn in Christ and supping at the Lord's table. Life's living towards dying is a passage into full communion with God.

51. The baptismal process can be seen as an "ordination" of the whole community to be a people exercising a "royal priesthood" for the sake of the whole world (1 Pet. 2:9). The baptized, together, come to share in the "triple office" of Christ as prophet, priest and king: witnessing, interceding and serving justice in the midst of the needs of all the world.

B. Christian ethics as baptismal ethics

52. As noted in paragraph 44 above, baptism signifies a special quality of Christian ethics which distinguishes it from other ethical systems and perspectives. We do not mean that Christian ethics does not have much in common with other ethics, in so far as other ethics also reflect our common human condition with its needs and our obligations to one another. But what we mean when we say that Christian ethics begins in baptism is that Christian ethics comes into existence only after repentance and forgiveness of sins and incorporation by the Spirit into the eternal body of Christ. The horizon of Christian ethics is no earthly city but the heavenly realm of God.

53. Christian ethics belongs to the mystery of the incarnation. Through baptism God makes a special claim upon the human being, a claim that ought forever to alter a person's moral vision. Baptism in Christ's death and resurrection is a daily event in the life of the Spirit. Daily we die into new life. Thus death is no longer the final horizon of human endeavour. Instead our eyes are opened by obedience to the everlasting life in Christ that God has secured through his own death on the cross.

54. A baptismal ethic is also an ecclesial ethic, not the ethic of the individual alone, but the fruit of the Spirit born within and through the koinonia of God's people. Baptismal ethics, indeed Christian ethics, is relational, not merely in the sense that it treats of our relations with others, but in that its inspiration and aspirations are rooted in the life of the community rather than just the individual.

55. Baptismal ethics affirms the pneumatological character of Christian life, an aspect which secular – and indeed some Christian ethics – leave out. The ground of our souls, washed clean with baptism and enriched by the blood of Christ, receives the gift of the Spirit and seeds of sanctification are sown within it. Thus a hymn of Charles Wesley beseeches:

Holy Ghost, no more delay;
Come, and in thy temple stay;
Now thine inward witness bear,
Strong, and permanent, and clear;
Spring of life, thyself impart,
Rise eternal in my heart.[15]

56. Through washing with water, and in some traditions anointing with oil, the church signifies God's own prevenient grace and our response – our turning away from evil and sin and towards goodness and perfection – which completes our adoption as sons and daughters of God. This adoption is the work of the Holy Spirit, as the Spirit is present within the sacrament of baptism (2 Cor. 1:21-22). As the Christians of Ephesus were told in the 1st century, those who believe in Christ are "marked with the seal of the promised Holy Spirit; who is the pledge of our inheritance towards redemption as God's own people, to the praise of his glory" (Eph. 1:13-14). This text is "enacted" in many baptismal liturgies and thus made visible, tangible, within the life of the Christian community. For example, the rite of baptism of the Church of South India, like the rites of many Anglican and Lutheran churches throughout the world, states that those who are baptized are *"sealed [by the Holy Spirit] as members of Christ, children of God, and heirs of the kingdom of heaven"*.[16]

57. The Spirit imparts itself with gifts of holiness and virtue. St Ambrose says simply that "all virtues... pertain to the Spirit".[17] A Byzantine theologian sums it up in this way:

> To those to whom he imparts of his own gifts, the Holy Spirit is "the Spirit of wisdom and understanding, the spirit of counsel and might and of godliness", (Isa. 11:2), and of the other gifts of which he bears the name.[18]

In some Christian churches these "gifts of virtue" are named and signified by the anointing or signing of the organs, senses or limbs of the baptized. Thus, for example, in the Roman Catholic Rite of Christian Initiation of Adults, the ears of catechumens are signed, *"that you may hear the voice of the Lord"*, the hands, *"that Christ may be known in the work which you do"*, and the feet, *"that you may walk in the way of Christ"*.[19]

58. Baptism is *metanoia* (repentance), a truly radical reorientation of personal existence so that life is lived always dying into immortal life with God. The ethic it brings into existence is a divine-human ethic, as each Christian and the entire church are reconciled to God and begin to participate in the divine life (2 Pet. 1:4). As Karl Barth states: "To those who are not ignorant, the sign of baptism speaks of death". He continues:

> Baptism bears witness to us of the death of Christ, where the radical and inexorable claim of God upon men triumphed... The void brought into being by the death of Christ is filled with the new life which is the power of the resurrection.[20]

Thus Christian ethics is the newness of life in Christ of which St Paul speaks, lived in the power of the Spirit.

59. Baptismal ethics is an ethics of martyrdom which outstrips the fear of losing one's life, so that death no longer overshadows and frustrates every effort to live life fully. Nicholas Cabasilas makes a remarkable statement about this in his 14th-century work *The Life in Christ*:

> For this is the end of baptism, to imitate the witness of Christ under Pilate and his perseverance until the cross and death. Baptism is an imitation by means of symbols and images of these sacred acts, *but also – for those who have the opportunity to risk their lives to show their religion – by the very same acts themselves*.[21]

Many Christians throughout history have, in fact, lived out their baptism in this way, in martyrdom. In the early church some martyrs were baptized by blood, dying before they received water baptism.

60. An ethic of baptism is both mystical and ascetical (cf. BEM, Baptism, para. 9). It is both liberation from sin and enjoining of responsibility towards oneself and others, a call to keep one's eyes on Christ and his kingdom, to struggle constantly with evil in oneself and in the world. Baptism is a call to holiness and perfection. But just as Christian baptism is not a classic "purity rite" (see para. 32 above), so this holiness is not the same as ritual purity. It is rather the surprising holiness of Jesus Christ, who was made "unclean" with us, who was with the outsiders and the ungodly in loving service, who suffered "outside the city gate" (Heb. 13:12-14) so that the world might be reconciled to God. Such is also to be the way of the baptized.

61. Baptismal ethics is a movement of divine and human will, grounded and surrounded in the mystery of God's freedom and love. We increase in maturity to the measure of the full stature of Christ (Eph. 4:13). But this growth can be completed only through obedience to God

and acceptance of the gift of the Spirit and the grace that baptism confers: "Baptism is both God's gift and our human response to that gift" (BEM, Baptism, para. 8).

62. The ethics of baptism is transformative. Nothing short of a transformation of heart and mind is sought (Ezek. 36:26-28). Through baptism we begin a life-long process of transformation into the life in Christ (Rom. 12:1-2), being conformed to his likeness from one degree of glory to another (2 Cor. 3:18). So, too, the church, which is the gathering of those who have been and are being transformed in heart and mind, is mystery and prophetic sign,[22] the vehicle of an ethic that witnesses to God's plan for the redemption of the whole of creation.

63. Christians do of course – and too often – betray their baptismal promises. History is replete, for example, with instances of Christians doing violence against Christians, as in Northern Ireland, the former Yugoslavia and most recently Rwanda. Sometimes the blood of the ethnic group becomes thicker than the blood of the Lamb – or the water of baptism. Such events contradict our affirmation that we are all baptized with the same Holy Spirit into the same Christ. So when we speak of baptismal ethics and the relationship of love with one another, we cannot pretend that we are fully faithful to our baptism. The Father's call to peace among humankind through the sacrifice of his Son and the gift of the Holy Spirit becomes a judgment that we must heed, trembling as we await Christ's coming in glory.

64. The vows of baptism point to the ethical task of making this world free from evil so that "the Spirit may abound" and may be known all the more. The ethics of baptism is finally mission in the world. While the kingdom of God is the horizon of our striving, the field of that striving is this world. In Matthew 28 we read of Christ's "great commission" to his disciples and so to the whole church. Jesus says: "Go therefore and make disciples of all nations, baptizing them in the name of the Father and of the Son and of the Holy Spirit, teaching them to obey everything that I have commanded you" (Matt. 28:18-20). This "great commission" may be seen as the summation and consummation of all the ethics that Jesus taught, and it is linked with baptism.

65. We have said at the beginning of this section that baptism makes Christian ethics both possible and necessary. But it is equally true that Christian ethics is fulfilled only if the church is in mission. This is what we learn from Matthew's text, and his message is all the more compelling when we note *where* Matthew tells us that Christ gathered the disciples in order to send them out into the world: "Now the eleven disciples went to Galilee, to the mountain to which Jesus had directed them" (Matt. 28:16). In this way Matthew reminds us of other events in

the gospel which are set on a mountain – where Jesus gave his commandments to his disciples (Matt. 5-7) and revealed his true identity (Matt. 17), leading us to affirm that baptism is truly an occasion of the ethics of the church.

IV. Conclusion

66. Recognizing the fundamental importance of baptism as "a basic bond of unity"[23] among the churches, this report has explored the ecumenical implications of our common baptism, in both its theological and liturgical dimensions, into the one body of Christ. We have considered the significance of the classic *ordo* (pattern or structure) of baptism shared by many churches today, suggested criteria for expressing the meaning of baptism in forms proper to local cultures (inculturation) and explored how the meaning and ritual actions of baptism are determinative for Christian ethical reflection and action.

67. We hope that our deliberations on the *ordo* (pattern or structure) of baptism may help the churches to move, where this is not yet the case, towards mutual recognition of baptism. We hope that our deliberations on inculturation may help the churches to understand the baptismal practices of others, as well as helping them to develop, where necessary, creative and responsible new forms of baptismal practice. We hope that our deliberations on the implications of baptism for Christian ethics may help the churches to find a common basis for their ethical reflection and action, as well as helping them to face together complex and potentially divisive ethical issues.

68. In worship at the fifth world conference on Faith and Order delegates affirmed and celebrated together "the increasing mutual recognition of one another's baptism as the one baptism into Christ".[24] Indeed such an affirmation has become fundamental for the churches' participation in the ecumenical movement. Yet the situation is complex, and sometimes more difficult than expected. It is not always clear precisely what is being "recognized"[25] – especially when the recognition of baptism does not mean admission to the table of the Lord. And of course there continue to be churches, including some deeply committed to the ecumenical quest, who in fact do *not* recognize the baptism administered by others.

69. Thus to Christians and churches who affirm the recognition of one another's baptism we ask: How far have we drawn the implications of that recognition, that common awareness of being claimed by Christ and belonging to Christ's one body? What does that recognition mean for our life together? How can it draw us to common confession, worship and witness? To Christians and churches who deny such recognition

we ask: What obstacles remain to our full recognition of one another's baptism, and how can we pray and work together to overcome them? And to all Christians and churches we ask: How can our baptismal practice express and nurture the degree of unity which is already ours as members together of the one body of Christ? What can we learn from our own baptismal experience, understanding and practice about that full unity to which Christ is calling us?

Recommendations from the consultation

Members of the consultation on "Becoming a Christian: The Ecumenical Implications of Our Common Baptism" affirm the central importance of worship within the ecumenical movement and in ecumenical study and discussions. We therefore recommend:

> *That the report of this consultation be widely distributed to churches, ecumenical groups, theological colleges, liturgists, pastors, theologians and ethicists for study and reflection.*

We affirm the importance of the Faith and Order study on the role of worship within the search for the visible unity of the churches and recommend to the Faith and Order Commission:

1. *That the study begun at Ditchingham and further developed at Faverges be continued;*
2. *That the ongoing Faith and Order studies on ecclesiology, hermeneutics, ethics and ecclesiology pay attention to matters of worship in general, and to the results from Ditchingham and Faverges in particular.*
3. *That the links which Faith and Order has begun to make with ecumenical liturgical groups (e. g. the Societas Liturgica, the English Language Liturgical Consultation (ELLC), and the Joint Liturgical Group) be furthered and developed.*

NOTES

• This text has appeared in *Studia Liturgica*, Vol. 29, No. 1, 1999, pp. 1-28, and the German translation has appeared in *Una Sancta*, 1/98, pp. 73-96.

[1] Scriptural quotations are taken from the New Revised Standard Version (NRSV) of the Bible, copyright 1989 by the Division of Christian Education of the National Council of the Churches of Christ in the United States of America.

[2] See Thomas F. Best and Dagmar Heller, eds, *So We Believe, So We Pray: Towards Koinonia in Worship*, Faith and Order Paper No. 171, Geneva, WCC, 1995.

[3] See the "report of the consultation", paras 45-49, *ibid.*, pp.15-16. Para. 49 notes the Commission's statement at its Louvain meeting in 1971 that "in all Faith and Order studies the importance of considering the subject in close relation to its expression in worship should continually

be remembered. Indeed sometimes such expression may form basic material *without which the study cannot yield fruitful results.*" For this see the Report of Committee II on "Worship Today", 5, in *Faith and Order: Louvain 1971: Study Reports and Documents*, Faith and Order Paper No. 59, Geneva, WCC, 1971, p.218, emphasis added.

[4] Report, para. 9, *loc. cit.*, p.8.

[5] *Baptism, Eucharist and Ministry*, Faith and Order Paper No. 111, Geneva, WCC, 1982.

[6] *Baptism, Eucharist and Ministry 1982-1990: Report on the Process and Responses*, Faith and Order Paper No. 149, Geneva, WCC, 1990, p.156.

[7] Report, para. 4, *loc. cit.*, p.6.

[8] Report, para. 7, *ibid.*, p.7.

[9] Report, para. 4, *ibid.*, p.6.

[10] Report, para. 36, *ibid.*, p.12.

[11] See para. 46 below for a discussion of this point from an ethical perspective.

[12] Report, paras 39-40, *ibid.*, p.13: "Liturgical inculturation operates according to basic principles emerging from the nature of Christian worship, which is:

a) trinitarian in nature and orientation;

b) biblically grounded; hence the Bible is one indispensable source of worship's language, signs and prayers;

c) at once the action of Christ the priest and of the church his people; hence it is a doxological action in the power of the Holy Spirit;

d) always the anamnesis of the mystery of Jesus Christ, a mystery which centres on his death, resurrection, the sending of the Holy Spirit, and his coming again;

e) the gathering of the priestly people who respond in faith to God's gratuitous call; through the assembly the one, holy, catholic, and apostolic church is made present and signified;

f) a privileged occasion at which God is present in the proclaimed word, in the sacraments, and in the other forms of Christian prayer, as well as in the assembly gathered in worship; and

g) at once remembrance, communion and expectation; hence its celebration expresses hope of the future glory and dedication to the work of building the earthly city in the image of the heavenly. In the process of inculturation it is important to consider seriously also those principles that are inherent in the church's liturgical tradition, e. g. baptism is normally administered during public worship, and eucharist is celebrated every Sunday."

[13] Report, para. 41, *ibid.*, p.14.

[14] "Hymn to the Holy Spirit", Mode VII, Armenian Rite of Holy Baptism, in *The Order of Baptism: According to the Rite of the Armenian Apostolic Orthodox Church*, Evanston, IL, St Nerses Seminary Press, 1964, p.51.

[15] "Since the Son Has Made Me Free", quoted in Geoffrey Wainwright, *Methodists in Dialogue*, Nashville, Kingswood Books, 1995, p.205.

[16] See *The Church of South India: The Book of Common Worship*, London, New York, Madras, Oxford UP, 1963, p.104.

[17] From his "Sermons on the Sacraments", cited in Edward Yarnold, SJ, *The Awe-Inspiring Rites of Initiation*, London, St Paul Publications, 1971.

[18] Nicholas Cabasilas, *The Life in Christ*, III, 4, tr. Carmino J. de Catanzaro, Crestwood NY, St Vladimir's Seminary Press, 1974, p.108.

[19] *Christian Initiation of Adults*, rev. ed., Washington, US Catholic Conference, 1988.

[20] Karl Barth, *The Epistle to the Romans*, tr. Edwyn C. Hoskyns, London, Oxford UP, 1933, pp.193, 195.

[21] *The Life in Christ*, II, 17, *loc. cit.*, p.94, emphasis added.

[22] See the Faith and Order study document *Church and World: The Unity of the Church and the Renewal of Human Community*, Faith and Order Paper No. 151, 2nd rev. ed., Geneva, WCC, 1992, pp.25-32.

[23] *Baptism, Eucharist and Ministry 1982-1990: Report on the Process and Responses*, p.51.

[24] Daily worship, Santiago de Compostela, 9 August 1993, in *Worship Book: Fifth World Conference on Faith and Order*, Geneva, Commission on Faith and Order, 1993, English: p.12, Spanish: p.32, German: p.53, French: p.74; cf. the Ditchingham report, para. 67, *loc. cit.*, p.21.

[25] See the papers and report from the 1996 consultation on "Baptism and the Unity of the Church", in Hvittorp, Finland, organized by the Institute for Ecumenical Research, Strasbourg, in cooperation with the Lutheran World Federation; and published in Michael Root and Risto Saarinen, eds, *Baptism and the Unity of the Church*, Grand Rapids, Eerdmans, and Geneva, WCC, 1998.

Bibliography on Baptism and its Ecumenical Significance

Compiled by the editors, with contributions from Janet Crawford and S. Anita Stauffer

This bibliography is not intended to be exhaustive. It gives a selection of recent secondary material on baptism, emphasizing ecumenical issues as well as views from various Protestant (including Baptist), Anglican, Roman Catholic and Orthodox perspectives. Most material is in English; but German and French sources (and one title in Dutch) are cited as well. For the most part, articles in dictionaries are not included.

For the texts of the church fathers concerning baptism, see particularly *Des mystères sacramentels* by Constantin Andronikof.

Aland, Kurt, *Taufe und Kindertaufe*, Gütersloh, Gütersloher Verlagshaus, 1971.

Andronikof, Constantin, *Des mystères sacramentels*, Paris, Éd. du Cerf, 1998.

Baillie, J., *Baptism and Conversion*, London, Oxford UP, 1964.

Baptême confirmation: bibliographie internationale 1975-1984, RIC supplément 99/100, Strasbourg, CERDIC, 1985.

Baptism, Eucharist and Ministry, Faith and Order Paper No. 111, Geneva, WCC, 1982.

Barkley, J.M., *The Worship of the Reformed Church*, London, Lutterworth, 1966.

Beasley-Murray, George R., *Baptism in the New Testament*, Grand Rapids, Eerdmans, 1984.

Beasley-Murray, George R., "The Problem of Infant Baptism: An Exercise in Possibilities", in *Festschrift Günter Wagner*, Bern, Peter Lang, 1994.

Beasley-Murray, George R., *Die christliche Taufe: Eine Untersuchung über ihr Verständnis in Geschichte und Gegenwart*, tr. Günther Wagner, new ed., Systematisch-theologische Monographie 1, Wuppertal, R. Brockhaus, 1998.

Benoit, André; Bobrinskoy, Boris; Coudreau, François, *Baptême, sacrement de l'unité*, Tours, Mame, 1971.

Blei, Karel, *De kinderdoop in diskussie*, Kok, Kampen, 1981.

Brand, Eugene, "Baptism and Communion of Infants: A Lutheran View", in Maxwell E. Johnson, ed., *Living Water, Sealing Spirit: Readings on Christian Initiation*, Collegeville MN, Liturgical Press, 1995, pp.350-64.

Brand, Eugene, "New Rites of Initiation and Their Implications in the Lutheran Churches", in Maxwell E. Johnson, ed., *Living Water, Sealing Spirit: Readings on Christian Initiation*, Collegeville MN, Liturgical Press, 1995, pp.292-309.

Brand, Eugene, "The Lima Text as a Standard for Current Understandings and Practice of Baptism", *Studia Liturgica*, Vol. 16, Nos 1-2, 1986-87, pp.40-63.

Browning, Robert L.; Reed, Roy A., eds, *Models of Confirmation and Baptismal Affirmation*, Birmingham AL, Religious Education Press, 1995.

Buchanan, C., *Anglican Confirmation*, Bramcote, Nottingham, UK, Grove Books, 1986.

Burnish, Raymond, *The Meaning of Baptism: A Comparison of the Teaching and Practice of the Fourth Century with the Present Day*, London, SPCK, 1985.

Chupungco, Anscar J., OSB, "Baptism in the Early Church and its Cultural Settings", in S. Anita Stauffer, ed., *Worship and Culture in Dialogue*, Geneva, Lutheran World Federation, 1994, pp.39-56.

Chupungco, Anscar J., OSB, *Liturgical Inculturation: Sacramentals, Religiosity and Catechesis*, Collegeville MN, Liturgical Press, 1992, pp.143-47.

Chupungco, Anscar J., OSB, "The Future Shape of Sacramental Celebration", in *Liturgies of the Future*, New York, Paulist Press, 1989, pp.102-39.

Church of Scotland, Special Commission on Baptism, *Biblical Doctrine of Baptism: A Study Document*, Edinburgh, St Andrew's Press, 1960.

Cochrane, Arthur C., "Baptism as the Basis of the Christian Life", *Journal of Ecumenical Studies*, Vol. 5, No. 4, 1968, pp.745-57.

Cramer, P., *Baptism and Change in the Early Middle Ages, c.200-c.1150*, Oxford, Oxford UP, 1993.

Crichton, J.D., *Christian Celebration: Understanding the Sacraments*, 3rd ed., London, Chapman, 1992.

Davies, J.G., ed., *A New Dictionary of Liturgy and Worship*, London, SCM Press, 1986, pp.55-87 (articles by various authors).

Davies, J.G., *The Architectural Setting of Baptism*, London, Barrie & Rockcliff, 1962.

Davies, J.G., *The Spirit, the Church and the Sacraments*, London, Faith, 1954.

Davis, Charles, "Today's Culture and the Meaning of Baptism", *The Ecumenical Review*, Vol. 39, No. 2, April 1987, pp.163-72.

Dixon, N., *Troubled Waters*, London, Epworth, 1979.

Duck, Ruth C., *Gender and the Name of God: The Trinitarian Baptismal Formula*, New York, Pilgrim, 1991.

Duggan, Robert D.; Kelly, Maureen A., *The Christian Initiation of Children: Hope for the Future*, New York, Paulist, 1991.

Eagen, Joseph F., SJ, *Baptism and Communion among the Churches: A Study of Three Baptismal Documents among the Churches in the Context of Faith and Order's Quest for Unity*, Rome, Pontifica Universitas Gregoriana, 1974.

Eastman, A.T., *The Baptizing Community: Christian Initiation and the Local Congregation*, Harrisburg PA, Morehouse, 1991.

Edel, Reiner-Friedemann, ed., *Die Bedeutung der Taufe für die Einheit der Kirche und den Kosmos*, Ökumenische Texte und Studien, Vol. 22, Marburg/Lahn, R.F. Edel, 1962.

Ehrenström, Nils, *Mutual Recognition of Baptism in Interchurch Agreements*, Faith and Order Paper No. 90, Geneva, WCC, 1978.

Elert, Werner, *Morphologie des Luthertums*, Munich, C.H. Beck, 1931-32.

Elert, Werner, *The Structure of Lutheranism*, tr. Walter A. Hansen, St Louis, Concordia, 1962.

Erickson, John H., "The Reception of Non-Orthodox into the Orthodox Church: Contemporary Practice", *St Vladimir's Theological Quarterly*, Vol. 41, No. 1, 1997, pp.1-17.

Erickson, John, "The Formation of Orthodox Christian Identity", *St Vladimir's Theological Quarterly*, Vol. 42, 1998, pp.301-14.

Erickson, John H., "Baptism and the Church's Faith", in Carl E. Braaten and Robert W. Jenson, eds, *Marks of the Body of Christ*, Grand Rapids, Eerdmans, 1999, pp.44-58.

Evans, Gareth R., *Baptism*, Norwich, Canterbury Press, 1986.

Fenwick, John R.K.; Spinks, Bryan D., *Worship in Transition: The Liturgical Movement in the Twentieth Century*, New York, Continuum, 1995, pp.135-45.

Fiddes, Paul S., ed., *Reflections on the Water: Understanding God and the World Through the Baptism of Believers*, Regent's Study Guide 4, Oxford, Regent's Park College, and Macon GA, Smyth & Helwys, 1996.

FitzGerald, Thomas, "The Orthodox Rite of Christian Initiation", *St Vladimir's Theological Quarterly*, Vol. 32, 1988, pp.309-27.

Geldbach, Erich, *Taufe*, Bensheimer Hefte 79, Ökumenische Studienhefte 5, Göttingen, Vandenhoeck und Ruprecht, 1996.

Gilmore, Alex, *Baptism and Christian Unity*, London, Lutterworth, 1966.

Goertz, Hans Jürgen, "Die ökumenische Einweisung der Täuferforschung", *Neue Zeitschrift für systematische Theologie und Religionsphilosophie*, Vol. 13, No. 3, 1971, pp.363-72.

Gounelle, André, *Le baptême: Le débat entre les Eglises*, Paris, Les Bergers et les Mages, 1996.

Haarsma, Franz, "Die Gültigkeit der Taufe in nicht-katholischen Kirchen", *Una Sancta*, Vol. 17, Nos 3-4, 1962, p.181.

Hamilton, David S.M., *Through the Waters: Baptism and the Christian Life*, Edinburgh, T&T Clark, 1990.

Hartman, Lars, *"Auf den Namen des Herrn Jesus": Die Taufe in den neutestamentlichen Schriften*, Stuttgarter Bibelstudien 148, Stuttgart, Katholisches Bibelwerk, 1992.

Hartman, Lars, *"Into the Name of the Lord Jesus": Baptism in the Early Church*, Studies of the New Testament and Its World, Edinburgh, T&T Clark, 1997.

Heller, Dagmar, "Baptism – the Basis of Church Unity? The Question of Baptism in Faith and Order", in *The Ecumenical Review*, Vol. 50, No. 4, 1998, pp. 480-90.

Heller, Dagmar, "'...ein Herr, ein Glaube, eine Taufe...'? Die Taufe in der neueren ökumenischen Diskussion", in *Jahrbuch für Hymnologie und Liturgik*, 36, 1996-97, pp. 58-65.

Holeton, David R., "Changing the Baptismal Formula: Feminist Proposals and Ecumenical Implications", *Ecumenical Trends*, Vol. 17, No. 5, May 1988, pp.69-72.

Holeton, David R., ed., *Christian Initiation in the Anglican Communion*, Bramcote, Nottingham, UK, Grove Books, 1991.

Holeton, David R., ed., *Growing in Newness of Life: Christian Initiation in Anglicanism Today*, Toronto, Anglican Book Centre, 1993.

Holland, B.G., *Baptism in Early Methodism*, London, Epworth, 1970.

Hubert, Hans, *Der Streit um die Kindertaufe: Eine Darstellung der von Karl Barth 1943 ausgelösten Diskussion um die Kindertaufe und ihrer Bedeutung für die heutige Tauffrage*, Bern, Peter Lang, 1972.

Huxley, Michael, "Baptism in Ecumenical Perspective", *Foundations,* Vol. 22, No. 3, July-Sept. 1979, pp.218-32.

Jagger, Peter J., "Christian Unity and Valid Baptism", *Theology*, Vol. 74, No. 607, 1971, pp.404-13.

Johnson, Maxwell E., ed., *Living Water, Sealing Spirit: Readings on Christian Initiation*, Collegeville MN, Liturgical Press, 1995.

Johnsson, William G., *Clean: The Meaning of Christian Baptism*, Horizon Series, Hagerstown MD, Review & Herald Publishing Assoc., 1980.

Jones, Cheslyn; Wainwright, Geoffrey; Yarnold, Edward, SJ; Bradshaw, Paul, eds, *The Study of Liturgy*, rev. ed., London, SPCK, and New York, Oxford UP, 1992, pp.111-83.

Jüngel, Eberhard, *Karl Barths Lehre von der Taufe: Ein Hinweis auf ihre Probleme*, Theologische Studienhefte 98, Zurich, EVZ-Verlag, 1968.

Karokaren, Anto, "The Relationship of Mission, Conversion and Baptism", *International Review of Mission*, Vol. 72, No. 287, July 1983, pp.344-64.

Kavanagh, Aidan, "Christian Initiation in Post-Conciliar Roman Catholicism: A Brief Report", in Maxwell E. Johnson, ed., *Living Water, Sealing Spirit: Readings on Christian Initiation*, Collegeville MN, Liturgical Press, 1995, pp.1-10.

Kavanagh, Aidan, *The Shape of Baptism: The Rite of Christian Initiation*, New York, Pueblo Publishing Co., 1978.

Kavanagh, Aidan, "Unfinished and Unbegun Revisited: The Rite of Christian Initiation of Adults", in Maxwell E. Johnson, ed., *Living Water, Sealing Spirit: Readings on Christian Initiation*, Collegeville MN, Liturgical Press, 1995, pp.259-73.

Kimel, Alvin F., "The Holy Trinity Meets Ashtoreth", *Anglican Theological Review*, Vol. 71, No. 1, 1989.

Kühn, Ulrich, "Sakramente", *Handbuch der Systematischen Theologie* 11, ed. Carl Heinz Ratschow, Gütersloh, Gütersloher Verlagshaus Mohn, 2d ed., 1990.

LaCugna, Catherine Mowry, "Baptism, Feminists, and Trinitarian Theology", *Ecumenical Trends*, Vol. 17, No. 5, May 1988, pp.65-68.

LaCugna, Catherine Mowry, "The Baptismal Formula, Feminist Objections and Trinitarian Theology", *Journal of Ecumenical Studies*, Vol. 26, No. 2, spring 1989, pp.235-50.

Lampe, G.W.H., *The Seal of the Spirit*, London, Longmans, Green, 1951.

Lanne, Emmanuel, "Baptism", in N. Lossky et al., eds, *Dictionary of the Ecumenical Movement*, Geneva, WCC, and Grand Rapids, Eerdmans, 1991, pp.75-80.

Lathrop, Gordon W., "Baptism in the New Testament and its Cultural Settings", in S. Anita Stauffer, ed., *Worship and Culture in Dialogue*, Geneva, Lutheran World Federation, 1994, pp.17-38.

Lathrop, Gordon W., *Holy Things: A Liturgical Theology*, Minneapolis, Fortress, 1993, pp.59-68.

Lathrop, Gordon W., "The Origin and Early Meanings of Christian Baptism", in *Worship*, Vol. 68, No. 6, Nov. 1994, pp. 504-22.

Lienemann-Perrin, Christine, ed., *Taufe und Kirchenzugehörigkeit: Studien zur Bedeutung der Taufe für Verkündigung, Gestalt und Ordnung der Kirche*, Forschungen und Berichte der Ev. Studiengemeinschaft, Vol. 39, Munich, Kaiser, 1983.

Lorenzen, Thorwald, "Baptists and Ecumenicity with Special Reference to Baptism", *The Ecumenical Review*, Vol. 32, No. 3, July 1980, pp.257-72.

Lumbala, F. Kabasele, *Celebrating Jesus Christ in Africa: Liturgy and Inculturation*, Maryknoll NY, Orbis, 1998.

Meeks, Wayne A., *The First Urban Christians: The Social World of the Apostle Paul*, New Haven, Yale UP, 1983, pp.150-57.

Metallinos, George D., *I Confess One Baptism...: Interpretation and Application of Canon VII of the Second Ecumenical Council by the Kollyvades and Constantine Oikonomos,* tr. Priestmonk Seraphim, Holy Mountain, St Paul's Monastery, 1994; see also the review by John H. Erickson in *St Vladimir's Theological Quarterly*, Vol. 41, No. 1, 1997, pp.77-81.

Meyendorff, John, "Baptême, confirmation et eucharistie", *Istina*, Vol. 17, 1971, pp.337-51.

Mitchell, L.L., *Worship: Initiation and the Churches*, Washington DC, Pastoral Press, 1991.

Moody, Dale, *Baptism: Foundation for Christian Unity*, Philadelphia, Westminster, 1967.

Murphy Center for Liturgical Research, *Made, Not Born: New Perspectives in Christian Initiation and the Catechumenate*, Notre Dame, Univ. of Notre Dame Press, 1976.

Nocent, Adrien, "L'initiation chrétienne", in *Le renouveau liturgique: Une relecture*, Paris, Beauchesne, 1993, pp.76-142.

Old, H.O., *The Shaping of the Reformed Baptismal Rite in the Sixteenth Century*, Grand Rapids, Eerdmans, 1992.

Osborne, Kenan B., *The Christian Sacraments of Initiation: Baptism, Confirmation, Eucharist*, New York, Paulist, 1987.

Panzram, Bernhard, *Die Taufe und die Einheit der Christen*, Freiburg, H.F. Schulz, 1964.

Papandreou, Damaskinos, "Zur Anerkennung der Taufe seitens der orthodoxen Kirche", in *Una Sancta*, Vol. 48, 1998, pp.48-53.

Pfatteicher, Philip H., "Baptism: Hallowing Life and Death", in *Liturgical Spirituality*, Valley Forge PA, Trinity, 1997.

Pigault, Gérard; Schlick, Jean, *Baptême: bibliographie internationale 1971-1973 établie par ordinateur*, RIC supplément 9, Strasbourg, CERDIC, 1974.

Ratschow, Carl Heinz, *Die eine christliche Taufe*, Gütersloh, Gütersloher Verlagshaus Mohn, 2d ed., 1979.

Root, Michael; Saarinen, Risto, eds, *Baptism and the Unity of the Church*, Grand Rapids, Eerdmans, and Geneva, WCC, 1998.

Roy, Kevin, *Baptism, Reconciliation and Unity*, Carlisle, UK, Paternoster, 1997.

Sava-Popa, Gheorghe, *Le baptême dans la tradition orthodoxe et ses implications oecuméniques*, Cahiers oecuméniques, Fribourg, Ed. universitaires, 1994.

Schlink, Edmund, *Die Lehre von der Taufe*, Kassel, Stauda, 1969.

Schlink, Edmund, *The Doctrine of Baptism*, tr. Herbert J.A. Bouman, St Louis, Concordia, 1972.

Schmemann, Alexander, *Of Water and the Spirit: A Liturgical Study of Baptism*, 2nd ed., London, SPCK, 1976.

Schnackenburg, Rudolf, *Baptism in the Thought of St Paul*, Oxford, Basil Blackwell, 1964.

Schneider, Theodor, *Zeichen der Nähe Gottes: Grundriss der Sakramententheologie*, Mainz, Matthias-Grünewald Verlag, 7th ed., 1998.

Schütz, Eduard, "Das leidige Gespräch mit den Baptisten über die Taufe", *Ökumenische Rundschau*, 1995, pp.194-207.

Searle, M., *Baptism and Confirmation*, Collegeville MN, Liturgical Press, 1987.

Sebastian, J. Jayakiran, *"... Baptisma Unum in Sancta Ecclesia...": A Theological Appraisal of the Baptismal Controversy in the Work and Writings of Cyprian of Carthage*, Delhi, ISPCK, 1997.

Singh, Godwin R., *A Call to Discipleship: Baptism and Conversion*, Delhi, ISPCK, 1985.

Smolik, Josef, "Baptism-Source of Witness", *International Review of Mission*, Vol. 74, No. 286, April 1983, pp. 214-16.

Steffens, Uwe, *Taufe: Ursprung und Sinn des christlichen Einweihungsritus*, Stuttgart, Kreuz-Verlag, 1988.

Stookey, Lawrence H., *Baptism: Christ's Act in the Church*, Nashville, Abingdon, 1982.

Stookey, Lawrence H., "Three New Initiation Rites", in Maxwell E. Johnson, ed., *Living Water, Sealing Spirit: Readings on Christian Initiation*, Collegeville MN, Liturgical Press, 1995, pp.274-91.

Strege, Merle D., ed., *Baptism and Church: A Believers' Church Vision*, Grand Rapids, Sagamore Books, 1986.

Torrance, Thomas, "Die Eine Taufe, die Christus und seiner Kirche gemeinsam ist, *Kerygma und Dogma*, Vol. 17, 1971, pp.188-208.

Vischer, Lukas. *Ihr seid getauft: Eine Untersuchung über Tauf- und Konfirmationsliturgien verschiedener Kirchen*, Zurich, EVZ-Verlag, 1961.

Vischer, Lukas, *Ye Are Baptized: A Study of Baptism and Confirmation Liturgies as the Initiation to the Ministry of the Laity*, Geneva, WCC, 1969.

Vorster, Hans, "Wir bekennen die eine Taufe zur Vergebung der Sünden", in Harald Becker, ed., *Was hast du, das du nicht empfangen hast? Festschrift für Eduard Schütz*, Berlin, WDL-Verlag, 1998, pp.21-35.

Wainwright, Geoffrey, *Christian Initiation*, London, Lutterworth, 1969.

Wainwright, Geoffrey, *Doxology: The Praise of God in Worship, Doctrine and Life*, New York, Oxford UP, 1980, esp. pp.124-27.

Wainwright, Geoffrey, *Worship with One Accord: Where Liturgy and Ecumenism Embrace*, New York, Oxford UP, 1997.

Wenz, Gunther, *Einführung in die Sakramentenlehre*, Darmstadt, Wissenschaftliche Buchgesellschaft, 1988.

Whitaker, E.C., *Documents of the Baptismal Liturgy*, London, SPCK, 1970.

White, James F., "Christian Initiation", in *Introduction to Christian Worship*, rev. ed., Nashville, Abingdon, 1990, pp.192-218.

Willimon, W.H., *Baptism: A Model for Christian Life*, Nashville, Upper Room, 1980.

Willimon, W.H., *Remember Who You Are*, Nashville, Upper Room, 1980.

Yarnold, E., *The Awe-Inspiring Rites of Initiation: Baptismal Homilies in the Fourth Century*, Slough, UK, St Paul, 1972.

Participants

Rev. Neville Callam (Baptist, Jamaica/West Indies) is a pastor, and lecturer in Christian ethics at the United Theological College of the West Indies.

Prof. ChangBok Chung (Presbyterian, Korea) is professor of liturgy at the Presbyterian College and Theological Seminary in Seoul, Korea.

Rev. Dr Janet Crawford (Anglican, Aotearoa/New Zealand), who teaches church history and liturgics in the College of St John the Evangelist within the Auckland Consortium for Theological Education in New Zealand, was moderator of Faith and Order's work on worship from 1991 to 1999.

Rev. Dr J.W. Gladstone (United, India) teaches theology at the Kerala United Theological Seminary in Trivandrum, India.

Dr Vigen Guroian (Oriental Orthodox, USA) teaches theology and Christian ethics at Loyola College in Maryland, Baltimore, USA.

Rev. Sen Kasek Kautil (Lutheran, Papua New Guinea) works with Kristen Pres in Madang, Papua New Guinea, and has been active in the Melanesian discussion of *Baptism, Eucharist and Ministry.*

Rev. Fr K. Joseph Labi (Eastern Orthodox, Ghana) is a member of the Mission and Evangelism Team in the World Council of Churches, Geneva, Switzerland.

Rev. Prof. Gordon Lathrop (Lutheran, USA), Schieren professor of liturgy and chaplain at the Lutheran Theological Seminary in Philadelphia, USA, is a past president of the North American Academy of Liturgy.

Rev. Dr F. Kabasele Lumbala (Roman Catholic, Democratic Republic of Congo) teaches liturgy at the Catholic Faculty of the University and at the theologate of the Oblates of Mary Immaculate in Kinshasa, Democratic Republic of the Congo, and is a member of the board of directors of *Concilium.*

Rev. Dr Jaci Maraschin (Anglican, Brazil) is professor at the Ecumenical Institute of Post-Graduate Studies in the Religious Sciences in Sao Paolo, Brazil

Dr Merja Merras (Eastern Orthodox, Finland) is lecturer in the Orthodox Theological Faculty in the University of Joensuu, Finland.

Rev. Dr Paul Sheppy (Baptist, England), minister of a Baptist church in Lancashire, is secretary of the Joint Liturgical Group of Great Britain.

Staff of Faith and Order/WCC
Rev. Dr Thomas F. Best (Disciples of Christ, USA)
Rev. Dr Dagmar Heller (United, Germany)
Mrs Carolyn McComish (Reformed, England)

Note: Travel difficulties prevented Fr Anscar Chupungco, OSB, of the Philippines from attending the meeting but his paper, as printed in this book, was read and made a major contribution to our work. Fr Chupungco is director of the Paul VI Institute of Liturgy in Malaybalay, Philippines.